Go

Glass of Wine

Linda Mason Crawford

"You will find purpose in your journey to fulfill your destiny and you will discover that getting there doesn't have to be so hard."

Linda Mason Crawford

Linda Crawford Books/ J & L Publishing

Linda Crawford Books
P.O. Box 23534
Waco, TX 76712
Facebook: Linda Crawford Books

Lindacrawford2@gmail.com

Scripture references in quotation marks are taken from the King James version of the Bible.

Linda Crawford Books/ J & L Publishing

Printed in the United States of America

Linda Crawford Books/ J & L Publishing

Acknowledgments

This book is joyfully dedicated to my husband, J.L. and to our four children, Jarrod, Jason, Ray and Stasha. You always believed in me, insisting that I have a ministry to share with the world.

To Dr. Arvis Scott, Professor of English at McLennan Community College, in Waco, Texas: Thank you for reading, editing, re-reading and re-editing this book, encouraging me in my writing skills, in my story-telling abilities, and in God's call on my life.

Acknowledgments

To Debbie Fultz, Professor of English at McLennan Community College, in Waco, Texas: Thank you for helping me with content and editing. Thank you for your encouragement and for enjoying my writing.

To Sam and Loretta Willis: Thank you for pushing me every other day for the last five years to get this book completed.

Acknowledgments

To my son, Ray Austin: Thank you for designing the book cover and for actually taking care of all of the publishing "stuff." Thank you for figuring out everything for me in my lack of technological skills.

To my Friends & Family: Thank you for the amazing support that you have shown in my quest to obey God; To Sue Connor & Sabrina Calhoun: Thank you for reading my script and for encouraging me to write more.

Acknowledgment to God

Most importantly, I thank God for trusting me and for giving me the wisdom and understanding that I needed to "Get it done!"

Contents

Introduction

I started writing this book over a decade ago, not because I wanted to, but because I felt that I was supposed to. The only problem was I didn't think I had anything to say. I often wrote unrelated notes in journals or jotted down a chapter idea. However, nothing became of those notes. I kept questioning God about the book's content and title. I felt at one time that the book would be about being married to an addict; after all, Christians are not supposed to experience such misfortunes, so I was, I thought, supposed to tell people how to overcome these hardships; still, that manuscript was never written.

I thought at one point that I would be writing a devotional about how to endure overwhelming situations, something that many people struggled with, but that manuscript didn't happen either. So I continued writing my notes, as I traveled to minister wherever God called me to. Some years into the journey, my friends, Sam and Loretta Willis, shared with me that they both felt I was supposed to write a book, and when I admitted to them that I knew that, they stayed on me about it. Every other week, one of them or both of them would say, "How's that book coming?" Thank God for people who believed in me, even before I believed in myself.

Through the years, as I ministered in different settings, I kept my ministry notes as well. I still had no idea what the book would be called and what its focus would be. Then it happened. Last year, I heard a voice say, "You need to get it done!" A few days later, my worship pastor, Jon Burleson, said he had a word for me, but he was hesitant to tell me. It didn't make sense to him, he admitted, but he wanted to be obedient. He said, "I feel like the Lord says I am supposed to tell you to "GET IT DONE!'" Well, needless to say, his words put a fire under me, so I started working diligently to "get it done!"

It seems instantly, things began to fall into place. I actually wrote an outline and placed my notes and ideas in appropriate sections. I was to write about destiny, giving practical tid-bits of wisdom to help people fulfill their God-given purpose in life. I had prayed so many times in the past about the title of the book, but when I finally got the answer, it made me nervous— *God, Destiny, and a Glass of Wine.* "Some people are not going to buy it because of the title," I said, as I talked to God about the book's title. But then I heard a very gentle reply. "And some people will buy it **because** of the title." So, here it is.

Recently, a high school friend whom I have not talked to in over 30 years sent me a Facebook message. She had seen announcements about some of the things God is blessing my husband and me to do. "Your life seems so full," she said, and she is right. Through the years, I hurt a lot, I loved a lot, and I learned a lot.

The two children that I reference throughout this book are both doing well. What Satan meant for bad has made them stronger. They are both pastors, leading godly lives. God has blessed me with a godly husband, along with his two, sweet sons. Our four children have families of their own, they are happy, and they are living life to the fullest. Yes, my life is full, and I am grateful.

I like to think that my book will help others have a full life, too. Over the years, I have learned lessons that I will never, ever forget. I am hoping that this book will do the same for you—teach life-long lessons that you will always remember. I have made many good decisions in my life because special people spoke into my life, but I have made bad decisions as well, because I did not know any better. Some things went over my head, some things went unnoticed, and some things just crushed me in my ignorance. It is definitely true that we will perish if we lack knowledge.

God, Destiny, and a Glass of Wine is not meant to be a quick fix for life's obstacles. It is not meant to be a "step one, step two, step three" guide. As a matter of fact, there is no set order for reading *God, Destiny, and a Glass of Wine*. You can read it in one sitting or skip around from chapter to chapter, in chunks or in tiny bites. The bottom line is no matter how you read this book, if you make an effort to embrace what it is saying to you, you will be changed—for the good. Be intentional about doing the exercises, writing in your journal, and noticing your circumstances. You can find clarity in your journey to fulfill your destiny, and you will discover that getting there doesn't have to be so hard.

Chapter 1

This too shall pass, but when?

I was almost out of breath by the time I made it to the car. Though it was just a few feet away, it seemed like 100 miles. I had parked my car in the back yard to hide it from the bank. Let's face it. It was an old piece of stick-shift junk, but it was all I had, and I was behind on the payments.

But tonight, in my panic to get out of the house, maybe the backyard wasn't so smart. Dressed in a gown, house shoes, and a thin jacket, I gripped the keys that were pinned inside my bra. Oh yes, my bra. I did have on underwear. That was the safest place to keep my valuables, like my car keys and what little money I had. I had learned a lot in my 29 years._With lightning speed, I dashed out the backdoor, tripping over the threshold, but still holding my balance and determination. Thank God my boy was spending the night with a friend. It was pitch-black dark outside, as I had no time to flip on the outside lights. I just needed to get out. Once inside my car, I let out a sigh, unaware that I had been holding my breath.

Quickly locking the car doors, I knew I was on my way. The car was run down and bent up, but it was my path to freedom tonight and my only means of transportation. I'll never forget it. It was a gray and black Toyota, well....a fading gray and a fading black, a hatchback, about 8 years old at the time, and a stick. Ha! A stick. That could be a holdup since I was still in the learning stage, but I could handle it. I tried to crank the old trap, but it just clicked.

I tried again, combining my efforts with a plea. "Please God, I need my car!"

Just as the motor turned over, I heard that dreadful sound, a swatch-type sound, like an old screen door dragging. My God! He knew I was going to try to get away. He knew, so he had unlocked the hatch back, ahead of time! He was in the back so fast; all I could do was bite my lip and jerk forward.

"Stop the car, Lynn, and give me the money!" he yelled, as he swiftly crawled into the back seat. He lurched through the bucket seats so fast that my head literally seemed to spin, like the girl in the Exorcist. Grabbing the steering wheel, he yelled again, "Gimme the money, Lynn!" The Exorcist...I was sure that his voice changed.

But tonight...no, not tonight. I kept driving, the car swerving across into the other lane and back again as he, too, gripped the wheel. We came within inches of hitting a minivan. I saw the headlights of an 18 wheeler that we also barely missed as we sped into the on-coming traffic. Hands pinned to the wheel, I was driving to my pastor's house, and no one was stopping me.

That was the life I lived for most of my 16 years of marriage to a crack addict, one that was much different from my single days of the quiet, country, church girl. I had never touched drugs in my life. I smoked only one cigarette that nearly killed me. And here I was, 29 years old, married to a drug addict. I had so many similar stories to contend with, jumping fences to get my car back from the drug dealers, standing toe-—to-toe and nose-to-nose with dealers who threatened to kill me if I didn't leave them alone about getting my car back, knocks on the door in the middle of the night from thugs demanding money my husband owed them, stealing my own car back and driving backwards, trying to miss the flying bullets. You name it; I just about dealt with it.

Many times over the years, I walked into my house to find that every piece of furniture and every appliance was gone—sold in exchange for drugs. I remember waking up one Christmas Day to find that my babies' gifts were gone, sold for drugs. Once, I frantically searched the streets of Tampa because my husband put our 6-year-old out of the car since it was "too dangerous to take him to the crack house," he said. This was before the days of cell phones. I don't even remember how I found my baby boy.

I could go on and on, but the only thing that matters is that one day, I accepted the truth that I had to forgive if I expected to move on with my life. I have since come to grips with the truth, that my now ex-husband was a good person, who loved people. When he was straight, he would give away his last. When he was not, he would take another person's last. I literally saw him take his shirt off and give it away. Once he pulled off his watch and gave it away, and then took my watch and gave it away, too. He had a heart of gold, but in addiction, he was the devil.

I had to find a way to forgive. I owed it to myself, my children, and my God. I don't remember actually knowing that. I mean, I knew, but not really. I was bitter and angry because of the years of hurt, devastation, and loss of things I had worked so hard to get. I was angry because there were people who said it was my fault that my husband was on drugs. They said I was exaggerating when I begged people to help him. I really thought if people acted like they cared, he would be delivered. In the meantime, we were going through hell, daily, until I just had to get out of the situation. Still, somewhere in my suffering and desire for God, I realized that holding unforgiveness was far worse than my husband's addiction. So....I made up my mind one day to just let it go. But it was not easy. I didn't know how to let go, and even though we hear people say it all the time, I don't remember one single person saying, "Okay. Let me tell you how to let it go."

So there I was struggling to figure out how to do what I knew I had to do. Through trial and error, I did discover that "letting go" almost always includes forgiving yourself or someone else before you can even begin to walk the path of your God-ordained destiny. I felt guilty for putting my children in the situations they were in, for staying so long, for watching them suffer and go without. I was angry with my husband for doing this to us, and that's not all. I was angry with God for not delivering my husband and with the people who always gave me unsolicited advice, usually saying that I should not end my marriage. One lady who heard from a lady who heard from someone else that my husband had an addiction, called me up to tell me if I would quit my job as a college professor, my husband would feel more like the head of the house.

Well, let's see. I had been there. I had done that. I had taken that advice before when we lived in Atlanta. "Just let him be the head," my well-to-do friend said. "He doesn't feel like the head because you work." Back then, I was desperate, so I tried that. Actually, it was the doctor's orders. My mom died while I was pregnant with my daughter, just eleven months after my dad died. I didn't handle it well. I was sick all of the time. I threw up constantly and I didn't have an appetite. The doctor put me on bedrest, so I couldn't work. But my unemployed status just didn't work out very well for us. We were out on the streets at least three times because the bills were never paid.

I remember one particular time that we were evicted. We finally found a place that would let us move in without a deposit with the promise of painting the interior of the "not so nice" duplex. On moving day, our friends came over to help us move, but my husband disappeared for two days. It was his payday, and I knew what was happening. He was spending his paycheck on crack. We were starting out in our new place the same way we were kicked out of the old one. Our friends helped us all day, but I couldn't do very much. I was about 8 months pregnant, and my son was 11.

After we were all moved in that evening, our friends left. I remember opening and closing the refrigerator several times as my son and I kept hoping to see something in it. We had water, meal, oil, onions, and three white potatoes. I boiled the potatoes, cut them up, added oil and smothered them in onions. Stewed potatoes! Then I made hot water cornbread. Hey, I am from the country, and I learned to improvise way back in the day. My son thought this was the best meal, but I was not only embarrassed that my husband did not help us move; I was furious that he was spending his check, knowing that we had no food. I had a right to be angry. I had a right to hold this hatred in my heart. It was my right! And we would live this way for another ten years before I finally decided that I had peace about getting a divorce.

But getting a divorce did not make everything okay. I had experienced serious bouts of depression, but I covered it really well. I constantly blamed it on my life with my husband, but finally, from my own experiences, not just with my ex-husband, I came to the realization that I had to admit my own short comings. I dealt with depression before my son was born, and I had dealt with depression in elementary school and middle school, even in college. I just did not call it that. I thought I was just moody sometimes. And when I became a Christian, I dealt with depression, long before I even met my husband. One day it hit me. I had to stop pretending that as a Christian, I was "all good" because God had healed me. I was not all good. I was not healed. For me, I had to first come to terms with the pinned up emotional healing that I so desperately needed. I had to uncover the real pain and the source of that pain. I had to admit that my pain was not all on my husband.

Many times, as Christians, we believe we should be "stronger than that." Often from past teaching or from a lack of understanding, we are convinced that as Christians, we should not come under the attack of depression or hopelessness. Sometimes we feel as if we deserve to be in darkness because we are not "living right," according to someone else's standards. Sometimes, we are embarrassed to talk about our feelings of sadness and despair and deep, deep depression. And to make matters worse, some of our Christian counter-parts accuse us of not seeking

God enough or of having sin in our life. As a result, we keep our struggles private and never experience the inner peace and joy that God has for us. We might have a slight glimpse of our future journey, but we can't enjoy each day. So many people, regardless of religious beliefs or backgrounds, don't realize that they need emotional healing. **I call this lack of knowledge, this lack of acceptance and of understanding, the Cover-up Scheme.**

This practice of covering up emotional pain will slow our journey toward our destiny, or even cause us to self-destruct, if it is left unresolved. In scripture, such pain resulted for some people, in continuous suffering for generations.

The scriptures call it "the broken hearted." Elijah, a powerful man of God, was brokenhearted and wished for death. David was brokenhearted and wished for death. Saul was tormented, brokenhearted and wished for death.

This pain, in the Bible often resulted from sin that was never dealt with. So people from generation to generation felt the pain of the fathers of the past. Of course, you have heard of generational sin or generational curses that have passed from one generation to the next. But all sin causes pain and trauma. And if left unresolved, it continues to cause hurt and pain throughout and down through family lines.

Consider David and Bathsheba. Now different versions define his actions differently. Some say, "He took Bathsheba," and "took" is translated as "rape." Then Amnon raped his sister, David's daughter, Tamar. Tamar begged her brother not to force her. 2 Samuel says she literally said, "What about me?"

In other words, doesn't it matter what this will do to me?" Have you felt that way before? You wonder if the other person thinks about what certain actions will do to you. I constantly begged my husband to stop doing what he was doing. Many times, I said, "What about me? What about our marriage."

Scriptures says Tamar begged Amnon not to rape her but he did anyway, and then out of guilt he turned on her. Can you believe that? He turned on her, and when David found out, he did nothing. Do you think David felt unworthy because of how he handled Bathsheba and the death of her husband? Do you consider these cover-ups, where no one deals with actions? They are swept under self-rugs, covering up emotions that cause extreme pain in everyone's life. The scriptures say as a result, Tamar lived a life of desolation and disgrace, totally out of range of her destiny.

But this pain did not stop there. Absalom was angry about what Amnon had done to their sister. Years down the road, Absalom had Amnon killed all because of what he had done to Tamar. What if their father David had dealt with the situation? What if Tamar had not been made to feel ashamed? What if Amnon had accepted responsibility for what he did? What if Absalom had dealt with his hurt and anger? But no one dealt with their emotional pain! What if?

Research shows some children and adults have negative memories of things that happened when they were in the womb. Some can remember things that happened when the mom was just a few months pregnant. Back in the day, my grandmother used to say to pregnant women, "You marking dat' baby." If they cried a lot, she would say the baby was going to cry a lot because the mom was "marking" the baby. If they were afraid of something, she would say they were training (marking) the baby to be afraid. Most of us didn't believe her, but often we found later that what she said was true. And now scientists and psychologists have done studies that show her beliefs to be true as well.

Studies also show that many times when a child experiences feelings of rejection, abandonment, low self-esteem, unworthiness, and unexplained sadness, even suicidal thoughts, that often the child was conceived under not so good circumstances or as a result of rape.

Even if the mom considered adoption or abortion but changed her mind, or just didn't want the baby in the beginning but changed her mind, according to research, the child often goes through the previously mentioned negative feelings.

Did you know that studies show that many people who experience emotional pain today most often experienced some type of trauma and/or rejection as a child.

The most common way the enemy attacks is through some type of rejection, self-rejection, fear of rejection, lack of self-worth and abuse, all of which usually result in that shameful word called "depression."

So often these emotions stand between us and our destiny because we cannot move on. If this is speaking to you, I want you to stop what you are doing and on a piece of paper or in a journal, think about these questions and write your honest answers, including the description of your pain.

Be honest with yourself as no one will see what you write.

1. **What is your personal definition of emotional pain or emotional hurt?**
2. **What is your first memory of emotional pain, such as rejection?**
3. **What was that person's relationship to you?**
4. **Are you aiding in the cover up scheme? What action hurt you but you constantly deny that it did or you just won't talk about it?** Write your answer out in detail. You will deal with this information later on.

Now that you have these hurts and emotions out in the open of your heart, we can move on toward the Steps to the Road to Damascus (Paul found deliverance here). Often our hearts are filled with hurts, unforgiveness, cloudiness...so much that it is hard to see ourselves having any kind of positive future. But there are things that you can begin to do that may start you in the right direction toward your happy place, your journey to freedom. There are no quick fixes or magic formulas. In essence, this chapter's objective is to help you own up and give up things that might be hindering your destiny.

First, don't sweep things under the rug. Acknowledge any hurts, and wrongdoings and talk about them to somebody, even to yourself if necessary. A counselor would be ideal. If talking is out of the question, begin to keep a journal and write about your feelings every day—EVERYDAY! Second, acknowledge the history of that hurt. I don't know of any situation now that did not have a history of a person of connection experiencing the same thing or something similar in the past but the pain was never brought to light. Find out what happened to that person who wronged you or what happened in that person's background, if you can. This will help you with the next step coming later. Major health facilities are now incorporating forgiveness in their cancer treatment plans. Some hospitals even have what is called forgiveness therapy that is used along with Chemotherapy. Why? Experts say unforgiveness affects the effectiveness of a patient's medication. Studies connect unforgiveness with just about every major disease known to medicine. That's biblical but scientists think they have uncovered something new.

Think of all of the women who are coming forward bringing to light their experiences of assault and harassment.

I personally know of a friend who was molested when he was just 8 years old, by his teenaged female cousins. He experienced so many hurtful situations when he was a child, and from people whom he trusted.

He died an early death, never walking in the promises that were his, never experiencing peace and joy, even in the best of circumstances. He was a brilliant young man, but his emotional pain was so deep that he never quiet saw his potential. He never felt worthy of the call on his life.

He never felt worthy of the family that God had blessed him with and often said people would be better off without him. Yet, no matter where he went, pastors and prophets would tell him about the promises that God had made to him. These people did not know him, but God always revealed to them the plan that He had for his life. They always laid out the same plan.

Had he confronted the issues in his heart, the pain he experienced since he was 8 years old, the loss of his baby brother of which he felt responsible, the contempt he had for his cousins who molested him and the shame he experienced all the days of his life, experts say this could have opened the door toward his healing and toward his walking in the plans that God showed him so many times. Find your person to talk to and write about the hurt as well. Ask questions to at least give you a little understanding into the why's or the how's of the person you need to forgive.

Then move on to another step involved in emotional healing, which is **understanding the real or whole story behind that person's actions**. Experts say that if you identify the person you believe contributed to your emotional pain, and you then make the effort to understand that person's story, you are taking yet another step toward your deliverance, toward your road to Damascus. Understanding, even a little bit, may help you identify with the abuser's own emotional pain, and thus move you toward **empathizing with that person.** Remember that with each breakthrough, you should be writing, even if you do have a person to talk to. Just write. You will write things that you won't say to your person. You will write things that you won't remember to say to your person. Just write. This, too shall pass. Forgiveness is the key.

Prayer: Father, You are the Healer of the brokenhearted. You promise to bind up our wounds. Because it is

YOUR nature to heal, I ask You to do just that in the name of Jesus. Heal the emotional wounds in my heart, right now. By Your love and power, remove the hurt and anger that I am experiencing. Help me walk in Psalm 147:3...to move on to emotional wholeness (Psalm 147:3), for you say that you heal the brokenhearted and bind their wounds. Thank you, Lord for setting me free.

Chapter 2

What you say is what you get!

I stood there in utter disbelief as I watched the man drive up in front of me. The big, old ugly truck was black and brown—black for the color and brown for the thousands of rust spots. As I climbed into the driver's seat, I struggled to reach the actual seat.

This had to be the tallest, biggest, ugliest truck that I had ever seen. But at least it was an automatic, I remember thinking.

I mean it could be worse. Driving down the interstate, I felt jarring and heard rattling that to this day, I cannot identify.

Every few miles, the driver's side door would come ajar while I frantically sought to prevent the door from swinging completely open in mid-traffic.

"Putting it to the floor," took on a new meaning for me that day.

Putting it to the floor literally meant pressing the accelerator with care trying not to get my foot stuck in the rusted out hole in the floor board.

Peering downward ever so often, I could see the pavement underneath the truck, as I tried to move faster than the 40 miles per hour that the truck allowed. I didn't dare look out the window at passing cars, for fear that someone would recognize me in the evil piece of rusty, noisy junk.

I finally made it across town, parking in front of my friend's house. She had picked up my 12-year-old from school while I tried to get my hands on some transportation. Thank goodness for my friend. We lived just a couple of blocks from each other, and we often picked up each other's kids from school.

Blowing the horn, I sat there, afraid to get out of the tall truck because I knew the struggle of trying to get back up into it.

I will never forget the horror on my little girl's face. Even from the street's distance, I could see the disbelief. The view was very clear, especially since all of the windows were down. No, not by my choice—they were just permanently in the "rolled down" position. I motioned for my girl to come as she stood there in the front door, glued to that one spot. She didn't ask questions, and she definitely did not run out to meet me with the usual hug.

"Mommy no!" she said in a loud, desperate voice. "I'll catch a ride," she said, as she quickly stepped back inside and closed the door.

Typically, that would not have happened. My kids always knew that I would not play around with their disobedience or disrespect.

Normally, "the look" would have spoken, and my daughter would have been climbing into the truck. But this was bad. It was really bad, and I let it be. I just couldn't see myself putting her through the embarrassment that was yet confronting me.

Quickly, I decided to let it go, so I made my way home, looking straight ahead, especially when I saw my neighbors working in their yards. But I had a plan. I would hide the truck in my garage, and leave early in the morning to park far, far away in the parking lot at my job. But soon an even greater shock came as I realized that I could not get the entire truck into my garage. It became clear to me why the company advertised, "No credit card needed." They knew no one was going to steal their cars and trucks, and they knew their cars wouldn't make it out of the city limits.

Have you ever lived off a credit card because you now have one income instead of two? Back in 1999, after I was divorced, I had an accident in my car and needed a rental car until my car was repaired. Even though I had rental coverage, I had to first pay for the car rental and then be reimbursed. Uh…problem. I had been living off my credit cards. I couldn't rent a car because I was over my limit on all of the cards. I ended up going to one of those places that says, "No credit card needed."

That day as I sat in my half hidden truck, I felt the anger rising. Enough is enough! I turned around sideways, with my feet dangling to the ground. I slowly slid out of the truck, but in doing so, I felt an overwhelming need to stomp my feet. By now I was crying and stomping uncontrollably. “Lord!” I cried out. “I am your child!” I immediately thought about the many times I convinced friends or acquaintance to call those things that are not as though they are. I knew I had to begin to change my words if I wanted to change my situation. Instead of saying I couldn’t get a decent rental because I couldn’t pay for it, at that moment, I started saying I was taking that truck back and I would get the best thing on the lot. Well, the best thing on the lot was still a piece of trash. So I changed my strategy and called my insurance company to see if they would pay first. I tried everything to get the rep to pay for my rental up front. I told her that I would wash her car, clean her house, and even babysit if she would just get me out of that big ugly truck. She laughed hysterically, calling me hilarious, but finally, she told me to go to Enterprise and get a car.

I began my confession again. "I will ride off that lot with the best thing that they have." The truth is I was on my way to pick up an economy car for one month while my car was undergoing a major repair. When I arrived, customer service informed me that all economy and standard cars were rented out because it was a holiday weekend.

The man continued that since it was not my fault, however, he would have to put me in what they had left on the lot, a top of the line Cadillac, "The best thing we have on the lot," he said. "But you will have to come back on Monday to pick up an economy car," he explained. Oh my goodness! I loved that black SLS, do much so that I wanted one of my own. I even saw one listed for sale in the newspaper. I looked at the ad so much that I knew the phone number of the owner. “This is my car,” I would say to my kids. “It is!” they replied.

Here’s the thing though. Each week when I returned the car that I was supposed to drive only until a smaller one was available, something went wrong, and I had to keep it.

Each time I would say, “I brought the car back but I know I’m going to have to keep it for another week.” Once the reps couldn’t find the economy car that they had reserved for me because, as they later discovered, they accidentally gave it to someone else. I left in the Cadillac. Another time, they had their last economy car reserved for me, but they couldn’t find the keys among those hanging on the wall. I left again in the Cadillac. And once, the rep told me that for some reason, her records showed that I was supposed to be in the Cadillac for another two weeks. Yes, you guessed it. I left in the Cadillac. In the meantime, my children were telling people that their mom was getting a car soon, "like the one she is driving." I was convinced, too, but common sense told me that I couldn't afford a new one. After a month of driving the top of the line car, that I spoke to life in faith, my car was ready. When I went to pick it up, it quit again, even before I drove it off the lot.

A few days later, my friend called and said he found a used car for me. It belonged to his neighbor. He had already talked to a banker and worked out the details for me.

He assured me that I would like the car though I had not seen it, and since I was not in a position to complain, I thanked him and went to the bank to sign the papers. Looking at the owner's phone number, I said to myself, "I know this number."

It turns out the car was the one that I saw in the paper a month before, that I had "marked" and spoken over.

Sometimes during our journey, we talk ourselves out of blessings that were certainly meant for us. We say things like, "There's no use in asking. They already said they won't do it." Well, the woman who wanted the crumbs from the table had asked several times, and yes, she finally did get a "Yes." We worry ourselves out of the answer that we need.

Some people say they will ask while at the same time, they declare the answer is going to be, "No." "I'll ask. All they can do is say, 'No.'" What! Why in the world would you say those words? Why not declare a different outcome. "All they can do is say, 'Yes.'"

Back in 1987 I talked to administrators at a Georgia university. They ASKED me to apply for a position there. I filled out the app (these were still the days of mailing applications) and put it in the car to take to the post office in Atlanta where I lived at the time. Then I got the call that my mom had passed away, just 11 months after losing my dad. Several days later, I was at home in Mississippi preparing to say good bye to my mom as the funeral was the very next day.

Then I saw it. The app was still in the car, and I had missed the deadline. Frantic, I called the department chair, hoping she was still in her office even though it was a very late Friday evening. She was there! She told me not to worry and to just mail it the next day overnight express so that she would be sure to get it by Monday.

Wow! What a break. My plan was to get up the next morning and go to the post office before the funeral. That was the plan. But that night during the family visitation, my mom's older brother told me that he didn't feel well. A few hours later, he had a heart attack and died. This was a nightmare, like a soap opera. Needless to say, we were all up all night, devastated, totally torn apart, and the next day, guess what I forgot.

The good news is I did get the job. When I did mail the app the following week, the committee accepted it two weeks late. They decided that there was just no way that I made up a story like that. I loved my job at GSU, but had I not asked for a second chance, I would have missed out. I didn't go into the situations with negative words. I simply asked. How many times have you spoken negative over a situation before you even knew the whole story? Who knew the committee would respond that way—saying they just didn't believe I made that up.

Folks, stop declaring chaos over your life or the life of your children, your marriage, or your loved ones in general. "What you Say is what you get!" Your words are important. They can bless you or they can stress you. Electricity can give you light, but it can also cause your death. Scripture says the tongue is the same. Proverbs 18:21 says, "Death and life are in the power of the tongue."

People laugh because I use the term "Happy People." I started that back in the day when I read that as a teacher I can set the atmosphere for my classroom. So I began praying joy over my students. It's amazing that I saw an immediate change in their attitudes.

"Good morning, Happy People," I say, even now, as I enter the classroom. If I forget, it never fails that one student will say, "Happy Teacher, are you okay?" I make declarations over myself and my environments every day, starting with the "Happy" statement.

When people ask me how I am doing, sometimes I respond with, "It's a great day to have a great day!" I have a daily declaration. "I feel great. I'm doing great. I'm walking in my destiny; everyday I'm taking the road less traveled.

I make the right decisions for my life because I lean not to my own understanding, but in everything, I acknowledge the Lord, and HE directs my path. He leads me, He talks to me, and he keeps me on the right track. I am strong, healthy, and looking forward to my future."

My husband declares over our lives, "Exceptional health! Extravagant wealth!"

I often tell my students who are declaring that they are having a bad day that I refuse to allow those one or two or three or four unexpected, not-so pleasant things that happen in a day, or a week or a year, or several years to dictate my day, or week, or life in general. I have the authority here. I have the say so here.

"The circumstance might slow me down a bit," I tell them, "but they don't dictate what my whole day will be like, or what my week will be like, and they don't dictate what my life will be like.

I made up my mind when I was delivered from depression, that circumstances would no longer control me. I control the circumstances with my words, my thoughts, and actions.

I am an overcomer because I choose to be. I choose to SAY that I am more than a conqueror through Christ Jesus. I choose to believe that I can do all things through Him who strengthens me.

I am not a victim unless I allow myself to be. I watch what I say because I know the truth. I don't focus on what reality says. I focus on what faith says. I pay attention to what I say, and I care about what the Word says. I know that I can frame my own world with my own words, and I choose to believe what the word says about me. I believe in calling those things that are not as though they are. I don't use the word "overwhelmed" because it has a major negative effect on me. I will admit sometimes that I am just a little "whelmed, but I will be alright."

A lady once told me that she could not grasp what I was saying. "I'm 55 years old," she said, "but if I declare that I am going to be Miss America, it's not going to happen." Well of course not. I'm not talking about crazy things like that or saying, "I don't like my husband, so I declare I'm getting yours." Of course, I have common sense.

Psychologists have been doing studies over the years about the effects of our words. They think they have come up with new information, but it's scriptural. Their studies show that if parents speak negatives over their children long enough—good or bad—eventually those children become those declarations. "You're good for nothing. You'll never amount to anything." The same holds true for anyone, adults included. In one study, doctors took two control groups, both with terminal Cancer, and studied the results of speaking positive affirmations to one group and negatives to the other. The findings showed that in every case, those who constantly spoke and received positive affirmations outlived the others, sometimes twice as long. They call that new information. I call it Bible information. Proverbs 6:2 says, "Thou art snared with the words of thou mouth." This scripture is actually talking about hanging yourself if you co-sign for someone you hardly know.

But I believe it's relevant to what I'm talking about today. The word, "snared" means to hold one in a trap. We entrap our lives or our circumstances with our words.

Many times, we don't think about what we are saying. We don't think about the impact of our words. Have you ever said something and wanted to take it back, but the damage was done when you said it? Have you ever said something, perhaps to one of your kids or even to your spouse or dear friend---something hurtful, something negative, and watched the recipient of your words just lose heart right before your eyes. Have you ever been the recipient of hateful, hurtful words that just literally tore you down, tore you apart?

Have you ever known a person who told lies and more lies and actually started believing them, and you did too! The words you speak over yourself or over your life have the very same effect on you!!!!! The words you hear or listen to have an effect on you---whether they are positive or negative. Faith cometh by hearing, and death cometh by hearing also. We once had a guest speaker who talked about a friend who, for whatever reason, was in a coma for several years. During that time, she was diagnosed with a very aggressive form of Cancer, but to the doctors' surprise, the Cancer never progressed. She remained in that coma, and the Cancer did not spread. Miraculously, she woke up one day, in her right mind, but the doctors felt they needed to tell her about the Cancer. Within a few weeks, the Cancer spread throughout her body, and she died. As long as she could not hear the negative words about her condition, she lived, but when she heard the words of the deadly diagnosis, she died. The tongue holds the power of life and death. Happy People, **What you say is what you get!** If you hang with negative people, you become like them. Birds of a feather do flock together. Positive begets positive. Negative begets negative. I always say when you run into a negative talking person, keep running.

One of my friends had a baby girl several years ago. She was born deaf, blind, and had massive calcifications on her brain. The doctors offered absolutely no hope, explaining that her condition was irreversible. They said she would never walk, talk, crawl, hear, or see—that she would do nothing except drool for the rest of her short life. The doctors wanted to admit her to a special facility but her parents said no. For one solid year, the family spoke over 100 healing scriptures and words over that child. When the mom changed her baby's diapers, I heard her say things like, "Kick for Mommy. You have strong legs to kick with and perfect hearing. You have 20/20 vision and you will walk. Your mind is perfect. You will live a long and healthy life."

Even though things in the natural became worse as the tests results were bad and medical reports were always negative, the family asked God for a change by the time the baby was one. Day after day, they said only positive things to and about their baby. Immediate family members did the same.

Friends did the same. They spoke only good things to their baby—all day, all night, and they stayed away from people who saw a blind, deaf, disabled baby instead of a healed baby. They wouldn't allow negative family members to see the baby.

Do you know what happened to this baby, a baby who could not move any parts of her body—a baby who would never move or crawl or see or talk or have a life, according to tests? On her 1st birthday, the exact day, she just got up with no warning and crawled. When she was 1 ½, she got up and walked. The doctors called her "the miracle baby." Today, she is a grown woman, a beautiful, smart, intelligent young woman, all because her parents used the power of the tongue, thoughts, and actions. They used their tongue to speak words that worked on their child's behalf. Remember: our tongue is like electricity—it can help us or it can kill us—depending on how we use it.

Are you guilty of speaking negative words over your own situation? "I'll never make it til the end of the week," or "I'll never be able to pay these bills," or what about this one: "I'm always broke—always have been—always will be." I very often hear people say, "Oh, I'm trying to come down with something," or "I'll probably get that virus. It's going around, you know." What about this one or words similar to this one? "Well you know heart attacks run in my family. I'll probably have one before I'm 50. All of the women in my family do."

Are you guilty of saying things like, "I can tell this is going to be a bad day," or "If it wasn't for bad luck, I would have no luck at all." Sometimes, I just can't handle it when I hear my acquaintances saying bad things about or to their children. "That boy is bad—just like his daddy." I once heard one of my friends talking to her 13-year old about not getting her chores done. "Lazy! You're just lazy, just like your daddy's side of the family."

In 1997, when we learned we couldn't get a particular house because we didn't have the 15 grand for the down payment, we talked about how we all felt a peace about the house being ours. We decided to talk about the house like it was ours. Note though that first we prayed, and after coming into agreement, we called those things which were not, as though they were. Our daughter, then 9, packed her toys and her Barbie dolls, explaining that when we miraculously got the house, we needed to be packed and ready to go. The house was not occupied, so we went by every Sunday and visualized and talked about what we would be doing in our house. I went by twice a week and practiced driving down the curvy driveway, and our friends went over to pray and declare that God was putting things in place.

Three months later, we moved in, without having the down payment. The owners had cash offers for the house, but they told us that in their hearts, they felt that they were supposed to find a way to put us in the house. Their hearts were turned toward us.

It won't be easy to always say the right things. But remember, you create your world with your words. Before I went through a divorce, I struggled with my words, with the reality of things that my husband was a substance abuser. I spoke the right things and did the right things, yet I had to watch my spouse practically kill himself from the choices that he made about his own life. I realize though that I was not dealing with my will alone. He had to make his own decisions, and my words didn't penetrate his strong will. I remember saying, "Lord, do whatever you have to do to get this man straight. Just two requests: Don't allow him to die and don't embarrass me."

Two months later, however, things were worse. So on one of my deeply, religious, unselfish days, I prayed again. "Do whatever you have to do, Lord. Allow whatever you have to allow to get him healed. Just don't allow him to die, and I don't even care about the embarrassment." Oh, I was deep that day. Shortly after, I was praying and I really felt in my heart that if my husband didn't get it together, all of Waco would know about his problem, and I told him so. He was a very proud man, and the possibility of people knowing about the addiction bothered him, but it didn't change things. Eventually, all of Waco did find out. I remember crying out, "Lord, why didn't you tell me that you meant Channel 6, Channel 10, Channel 25?"

When his situation hit the news, I was stressed, embarrassed and depressed. I hid out and cried. I was soooo embarrassed, so torn. It was my perfect opportunity to fall back into the depression I had been delivered from several years before.

The next morning, I lay in bed, literally paralyzed with shame and depression. "Lord! I know I said I didn't care about the embarrassment, but I didn't mean it! Last week, when I was mad at him, I told you to kill him, and you didn't take me up on that! Why you wanna' listen to me now?"

Finally though, I came to my senses, and I began to talk to myself. I told my legs that they would move, that they would walk. I told myself that I had the mind of Christ and that I had perfect peace because my mind was focused on the Lord. I literally picked up each leg and threw it across the edge of the bed and yelled, "Walk!" I forced myself to do what I knew I had to do.

I have shared this story often, and every now and then someone tells me that I don't understand. "I've been this way for so long. It's just the way I am." One lady told me she had been negative all of her life and could not change. Not so. We can all change. You can have a better life. You can use words to speak life over yourself and your family, instead of death. My associate pastor read a quote that said something like, "I can't go back to change the past, my friend, but I can start today to change the end."

I grew up hearing that old adage, "Sticks and stones may break my bones, but words will never harm me."

What a lie! The kids in school always made fun of me because I was from the country. They made fun of me because we didn't have inside plumbing. Sometimes, my nickname was "Outhouse."

They made fun of me because I was tall and skinny and had long arms, and they made fun of me because I made "A's." They called me "Skinny Minnie," and "Olive Oil." Every day was a challenge for me, but if words couldn't hurt me, why did I cry so much when the kids' words hurt my feelings?

Words heal and they hurt. Scripture has a lot to say about our words. Proverbs 21:23 says we can get ourselves in trouble with our words. Proverbs 18 says our words (tongue) can heal us or they can kill us. James 3:3 says our tongue determines our path in life, and Matthew 12 says we are justified by our own words and condemned by our own words. **What you say is what you get.** Don't miss out on the plans that God has for you because of what you say or the words that you take in. Change!

In case you are thinking that you don't know where to start, let me offer you some guidance—what I call the 3 C's. **First, be willing to change your consciousness of the situation.** We have to become word conscious to change our confession, which will eventually change our lifestyle. Many times we have been hurt, so we continue rehearsing what that person has done. We say we've forgiven and we're fine, but we continue using idle words.

Have you ever had a sore that scabbed over rather quickly, but it was still sore underneath? Every time you bumped it, it hurt because it was not really healed underneath? Did you become more conscious of that area of your body? Did you make an extra effort to be more careful to avoid bumping the area? Did you become intentional? So it is with our hurts, our habitual negative words, or negative actions.

We must make an extra conscious effort to change our thinking and thus our speaking and actions. No one can change for you. You are on your own to simply STOP saying and DOING the things you have been saying and doing. You will need to make a conscious effort to spend more time in the word, and more time reading positive confessions so that your word consciousness becomes second nature to you. **Pull out your journal. Be truthful to yourself. Think about** the negative words or phrases that come out of your mouth. **Write them down.** You might write over a period of days as you remember some to the "death" words that you say.

The second "C" means change your confession. As you spend time being intentional about your words, now you must be intentional about the positive words that you say. **Pick up your journal and look closely at the** words and phrases that you wrote. Now for each one, **write a positive confession**. You can study and choose relevant scriptures or you can simply write positive affirmations that you feel in your heart. If you need help, turn to the Internet. Look up "positive affirmations" if you don't want to do scriptures.

The bottom line here is that you need to replace the old with the new. **Recite these** affirmations every day. **Put them on notecards or sticky notes** and **put them on your mirrors or in your car on the dashboard**. The objective is **to read** these statements several times a day on a daily basis.

Even before you see a change, you must continue to make your positive confessions. You have to faith it til you make it. You have to act it til you fact. You have to speak it til you see it. It doesn't matter if you are saying something that you don't yet believe. You must make confessions until they become real to you. When Jesus cursed the fig tree, he didn't hang around saying, "Oh, God! It hasn't changed. Look! It's still green!" No! He walked away from it, but first things, first. In any situation, you must seek God's direction for your situation. You must be willing to accept the fact that your desired end result may not be what God's end result is. At any rate, start out by doing your part. In faith, do what you know to do, and sometimes what you don't know.

Some years back, my friend was struggling because her husband was having an affair. Every Friday night, he dressed up, put on his cologne, and left for the weekend, but as hurt as she was, she refused to give up on her marriage, declaring that she wanted to fight for her marriage. So we talked about how she should use her words to curse that affair and command it to dry up from the root. The scripture says the fig tree started drying up FROM the roots, not to the roots. There's a difference. That means Jesus didn't see it changing because the change started underground out of sight, but it was still changing. "When he's getting dressed to leave," I said, "instead of yelling at him that he's tearing the family apart because he's having an affair (He knew he was having an affair by the way, so she didn't need to tell him), keep your distance and continue speaking and framing your marriage with your words."

I told her to go into her prayer closet or bedroom or wherever she spent her prayer time and begin to declare a new confession. "It doesn't matter what it looks like. That tree is dying from the root." When I told her to think of something else that she could do as an act of faith as well, she decided that she would set the table every Friday evening, believing that one day, her husband would be home with her eating dinner with his family. She also wrote out relevant scriptures and recited them daily. "Thank you Lord, that my husband is righteous. He walketh not in the counsel of the ungodly, but his delight is in you, Lord." "He, according to Eph. 3:19, is filled with all of the fullness of you, Lord, and his cup runneth over with holiness." "Thank you Lord, that He loves me as Christ loves the church."

You see she didn't just want him back home. She wanted him in church, actively involved and in love with Jesus. This woman was determined to save her marriage, to walk in the destiny that she believed was hers, but her journey was not easy. Many times over the next two years, she called me crying, even saying that she was tired of fighting. However, she always got herself together and continued speaking life over her marriage. It was a slow and hard process, but she eventually began seeing little changes. He would buy her a gift, every now and then, and instead of coming home on Sunday nights, he started coming on Sunday mornings.

Then he began coming home on Saturdays, and one Friday evening, she called to tell me he didn't leave and was having dinner with the family at the table where she had set a place for him for the last two years. When we last talked, he was in church, at home every night and in love with Jesus, his wife and his children.

The final "C" is that you must change the company you keep. Yes!

You need to examine your buddies, and if you cannot say that they make you better, perhaps you should consider spending less time with them. My friend hung out with friends who were divorced. They were constantly telling her to give her husband a piece of her mind. "Leave him," they said constantly.

Even when she shared with them that she was going to fight for her marriage, they constantly talked against her decision. They made it really hard for her to feel good about her decision.

Finally, she realized that she really did need to leave them alone, at least while she was on this journey. She needed to surround herself with people of greater faith, of tried experiences, of victories won, of knowledge in the Word to raise her back to life. She needed to hang with those who would speak into her life to give her that push that she needed to hang on just one day at a time.

Just give it a try. **Change your consciousness** by being intentional about changing. **Change your words** by watching what you say. **Keep** your affirmations before you. **Change the company** that you keep by choosing your acquaintances wisely, according to the words that they say. **Always be mindful** that what you say is what you get. And when you run into a negative person, KEEP RUNNING!

Chapter 3

You better recognize!

She met me at the door with a desperate look on her face. She seemed anxious for a 4-year-old, nervous, jittery. "I didn't do it," she said. "I didn't do it."

"You didn't do what?" I asked, picking up a bit of her nervousness.

Pointing to the bathroom, she said it again. "I didn't do it."

My kids had strict instructions on what they could and could not do, especially now that our water had been turned off. I had bought a 32-gallon garbage can, brand new, so it would be clean. Each night, when it was plenty dark, the three of us rode to my friend's house to fill the can full of water. That was our bath water. My kids knew how to lather up all over and rinse, without wasting a drop of water. We had clean, plastic jugs for our drinking and cooking water, and we had two other pails for our flushing water. We had rules. We had to do everything that we could to make all of the water last until it was time to "borrow" water from my friend again.

Walking toward the back door, I could hear my son singing and praying in the spirit. Outside! What the heck! It was broad daylight, and there he was with the flush pail, placed perfectly under the hydrant.

From inside, I could hear his singing, and through the screen door, I could see his hands raised high to the sky.

"I praise you, Lord. I magnify you, Lord. Thank you, Lord, for the water. Thank you God for your faithfulness!" He was dancing and waving his hands, as if he were all alone.

He wasn't. Our neighbors on both sides had a clear picture of their weird neighbors' activities. One neighbor was repairing his roof, and the other was raking her leaves. However, both had ceased to engage in their own business in the light of the entertainment going on in our yard.

"What are you doing, boy?" I said as I tried to pretend outsiders were not really starring at us. "Are you out of your mind? People are starring at you, dancing around like you don't have good sense. What's wrong with you?"

My boy stopped his prancing just long enough to explain. "Mom, you said we can praise our way out of anything. You said when our back is against the wall, just praise Him."

My son continued to explain that he had to use the bathroom but didn't have flush water. So he turned to God to fill the bucket with water. He decided to turn on the faucet and believe God would fill the pail.

Oh my gosh! Talk about being a fanatic, and in front of our neighbors who already thought we were just a bit different. By now, my daughter had eased her way outside.

"That's what you always tell us, Mom. That's what you say. Just praise!"

How embarrassing this was, and we had other rules, as well. Rule number 1: This is a family secret, to be discussed with no one. I trusted my kids; though they were 15 and 4, I knew I could trust them. Yet here we were outside for all to see, prancing, praying, and looking ridiculous.

Often, I felt my kids took care of me. My husband and I were separated because he was on his drug binge, and IRS was taking a big chunk of the only salary that we had—mine. My husband took care of those things, but it turns out his tax preparer was shady. They worked out deals where tax refunds went to the preparer's office, and after his cut, my husband took the rest for drugs.

The only problem was the refunds were overpayments, overpayments which I knew nothing about until the IRS garnished my check. My husband, of course, didn't have a job at the time, so as usual, I was the target. Plus, he had left the city, running from the law because of the bad checks he had written.

We were survivors though. My children were way too adult to be kids. They were analytical, always thinking about how to make things easier for Mommy. And through this rough time, we pulled together to make it work. We made our lives work. Our small house was our home, our refuge, and our stability. We had lights, a little food, and shelter. We were driving my colleague's car because the drug dealers had ours, and we were living from day to day. I clung to the scripture, "I have never seen the righteous forsaken, nor his seed begging bread." I struggled to make sure my kids didn't know how bad it really was, but when our water was turned off, of course, they had to know.

So we had rules. They were not to talk about our business and our struggles, and they were not to use the bathroom without flush water! Thinking back, I wonder how I figured they could control that. Surely, I got my wakeup call that day when it was obvious that my son had broken that particular rule. What seemed like hours was really only minutes. My children believed me. They believed in how I lived my life, on faith and on praises. Often one quick, seemingly minor decision can have life-long effects. My babies were used to living by faith, in good times and in bad times.

So as I thought about how my decision could possibly affect them for life, and not in a good way, I did the only thing that I could do. I lifted my hands to the sky and began to praise God. Within minutes, the three of us were praising God with all that we had, and within minutes, the hydrant began to make noises, jerking noises, as if it were engulfed by the force of a strong wind, but our water had been off for nearly two weeks. What was happening?

Standing perfectly still, we stared as water began pouring into the flush bucket. The flow was so strong, so powerful that it looked like dangerous flood waters pouncing on the inside walls of the pail. And then it stopped. The water spilled over from the top of the bucket, and the hydrant shut off.

Through the years, we have told that story many times. Of course, we know that some people don't believe us, but that's okay. We recognize God's hand in this situation. I recognized the doors that were opened and also the doors that could have been shut then and in the future, especially for my children.

You see, in our quest for knowledge and direction, we must recognize opportunities. I had the opportunity to build my children's faith even more, or I had the opportunity to shut them down. My babies experienced a miracle that day because I decided to practice what I had preached. In a split second, I realized these memories would be a part of their destiny, whether positive or negative. Often, in our search for our purpose, or in our influence on others, we fail to recognize the significance of our "right now" actions. My friend who let me borrow her car, used to tell her kids not to ever do anything they didn't want the world to know about.

We must be able to discern those things, big, small or what we often label as insignificant—for what they are. That one "thing" may be the thing that puts us before kings and queens and onto the path that clearly shows us what God has purposed for our lives. But that one "thing" could also be the thing that the enemy intends to use to cause us to go down the wrong path.

Scripture says to seek God in all of our ways; lean not to our own understanding, and God will direct our path, but he will not force himself on us. We must be willing to seek him. We must be willing to lean on his decision-making for our lives. We must be willing to allow him to direct us, as the word says God will bless our plans. I didn't have time that day to go to the Lord in prayer, to ask him if we should be acting a certain way in front of our neighbors.

Now, please understand that I don't believe Christians should chase a non-believer away because their "Christian" ways are so ridiculous. My choir directress used to say, "Scripture says we are a peculiar people. It didn't say we are odd." I also don't believe in serving God somebody else's way. This is my life and my Christian walk.

Yet, in a split second, I had to think about the future of my children. Could my actions actually cause them to lose faith in God? The enemy was on it, and I had to recognize that fact. I have often heard people say, "What's for me is for me," and that is true, but does knowing it mean it is going to happen regardless. The bottom line is God has a purpose for us. He has blessings with our names on them, but his promises come with conditions. We promise our children to give them certain things, but sometimes there is a condition. They have to keep their grades up. They have to stay out of trouble. They have to get their chores done. In my case, I had to activate my faith in God before men, my neighbors, and move on with my happy life.

I had to recognize the opportunity before me as a choice that could affect my life and my children's as well. I don't believe in coincidences. I believe in "God"ci-dences. Scripture tells us that our thoughts can be tamed, but to begin the taming process, we must first recognize that they **need** to be tamed. "Whatsoever a man thinketh, so is he."

Pick up your journey, and after giving this some thought**, write about a situation right now that troubles you a bit. Write about it in detail. List some of your options for settling this challenge.**

Now list the possible consequences for each of your listed options. **Briefly explain how each option might affect others in your life. Read this list often until you have peace about your decision.**

Studies show that there are no neutral thoughts. They will either speak life to us, or they will speak death to us. Experts say there are no "in betweens." If you think like a doubter, you become a doubter.

If you think like a winner, you can become a winner, but first you must recognize that ability within you. You can choose what you will be in this life.

Every thought has an effect—negative or positive. We have to "recognize."

Prayer: Father, help me to recognize your doors of opportunities. Help me discern the God in situations. I thank you, Lord.

Chapter 4

Fine! But don't do "IT" again!

The cold winter chill was angry. Four times I slipped on the ice, nearly losing my balance. Others stood around, chit-chatting now and then. Truth was no one wanted to talk. We wanted a warm blanket, warm hands and warm feet.

Where could it be? What was happening? Tiny drops of rain began to sparkle on the already icy surface as the fearless, fierce Hawk engulfed us, quietly, quickly and with a vengeance no man could even imagine.

Looking down, I saw my colorless hand. They weren't even red! No color? How could that be? Did that mean I was dying? I tried to wrap my thin, plastic coat around me a bit tighter, but it was cheap, evil really, nothing close to something that would keep me warm. Sliding my hands back into my pockets, I imagined us all being rescued. We all huddled under the covered area, including me. We didn't know each other but we felt a closeness. Yes, we were in this together, bonded strangers, friends forever.

One guy was really small, with an adult face, but a kid's body, it seemed. He had to be in his early twenties, but he was no more than 5 feet tall. His trembling body reminded me of a helpless child. He was so tiny, but in good spirits. His companion was taller, very thin, even with a thick coat on. I thought she was his girlfriend but later heard her say they needed their mom. Protector, yes one girl seemed to have the personality of a caregiver. She was constantly touching each of us, as if to say, "It's okay." The other guy, the quiet one, was just there. He never said a word, not one word.

Why was it so quiet, so deserted? Had we missed the Rapture? Suddenly, a car appeared, actually two cars. My new buddies screamed.

The tiny guy and his sister recognized the driver, a distant cousin I assume, as his sister couldn't remember the cousin's name. What did it matter, though? This was a miracle. This was God!

"Get in!" the cousin yelled, almost as quickly as the other driver yelled to the other two. By name! Did I say by name? The second driver called two names as they grabbed their backpacks and headed to the car! This was so exciting. We would be warm soon, cuddled in the heat of a nice, dry car.

Quickly the doors began to slam shut, blocking the sounds of laughter and thanksgiving, and I was the lone survivor. What was I thinking? I didn't have cousins here. I didn't know anyone except my roommate who took me in. My friends were hundreds of miles away and I was alone in this barren land.

Warm tears spilled over my eyelids. They left me. We were close, but they left me there, shivering and alone. We were friends. "Get in closer," the little guy had said earlier. "You're still in the rain." Everyone moved closer so I could squeeze in. Protector even put her hand on my shoulder ever so gently.

"Yeah. Come in closer. We'll use our body heat."

Standing there alone, I prayed, and then I cried.

Then, almost like magic, I saw it—the dark colored very nice car slowly approaching. "Oh my gosh. Someone is coming for me."

"Get in," the nice man said, as he rolled down his window.

I hesitated. I didn't know this man, but as I struggled to make my stiff fingers grip my backpack, in an instant, I knew it didn't matter. I slid into the front seat of the Cadillac letting the warmth embrace me. But as the door slammed, I saw them, immediately—the gloves— thick, black leather gloves. "Of course," I said to myself, as my senses came back to me. "It's 25 degrees out here. I would be wearing them too, if I had them."

Still, I felt an uneasiness, almost sick to my stomach, much worse than I felt minutes earlier in the cold and rain.

"Thank you so much, Sir, for picking me up. I was so cold."

He nodded his head and stared at the road, "driving cautiously on the ice," I said to myself.

"The bus didn't come," I explained. "I have a class in 45 minutes, but the bus didn't come."

Starring straight ahead, he made no sound, gave no nod, and made no eye contact.

"I go to JSU, you know. I'm a senior transfer. Do you go to JSU, too?"

"No."

"Do you teach there?"

"No."

"Oh. Ok."

My eyes seemed permanently glued to his hand, the gloves, firmly gripping the steering wheel. This did not feel right. Something was off. Panic set in, and I knew my miracle ride was not like the others.

"Why did you pick me up?" I asked softly. I could hear the shakiness in my words, dreading the answer even before his lips formed the words.

He turned to look at me for the very first time. “Have you ever heard of the leather glove trick?”

Slowly wiping the long stream of water that was now uncontrollable, I shook my head.

“Yep! I can do whatever I want—rape you, cut you, and dump you in the ditch. And who will know? I have on gloves, Honey.”

I felt my body trembling, shaking, as I tried to disappear into the softness of the leather.

Suddenly I grabbed his knee, begging, crying, fearing for my life. “You have to understand. I have a four-month old baby boy. Please! Please!”

I went on and on, not realizing that by now I was screaming, totally out of control. I could hear him telling me to shut up, but the words just wouldn’t stop.

"Shut up!" he yelled in a loud stern voice. "I'm taking you to JSU But let this be a lesson to you! Don't get in the car with somebody YOU DON'T KNOW!"

Years have passed since that dreadful, cold, winter day. My baby boy is almost 42 years old now, but I remember that day just as vividly as if it happened last week.

That experience made an impact on me, one that is with me today. It played a part in shaping my thinking, and it has helped to give me a clearer picture of who God is.

I think that man was an angel in disguise. People say we should find the good in everything and scripture says there is a purpose and a time for everything that "All things work together for good for those who love the Lord and are called according to his purpose." All things.

Often though for some, they never see the good behind crazy situations. Though I was young back then, somehow I knew that that pickup had a purpose. You see, hitchhiking was not new for me. Back in my days at another college, before my transfer, my friends and I used to do it all the time. We did it for fun. The college was out in the boonies, but we managed to get wherever we wanted to go, by hitchhiking. Once two guys picked us up to supposedly take us to the mall that was 20 miles away; instead, they drove in the opposite direction.

The only problem for them was that they were two and we were four—four silly, college girls who were ridiculously fearless. We laughed at them, informing them that unless they had guns, they didn't scare us one bit, and even if they had guns, we reminded them that they were two and we were four. Isn't that just like the enemy, to give us a false security in our dangerous, stupid decision making? The enemy's objective is always to take us out, to divert us from our destiny by whatever means necessary.

After putting up with our arrogance, loud threats, and girly, fear free chatter, the two young men finally realized we were having fun with them. Evidently, for them, part of their thrill would be our fear and helplessness. When it became apparent that we were not in that frame of mind, they abruptly stopped the car in the deep countryside and put us out.

The walk back to campus was a long, tiring one, but we were so oblivious to our ways that we didn't even know that we shouldn't share our story with the wisdom of an older adult. Our dorm matron was not impressed and made us listen to her long lecture about safety, stupidity, guns and death. But this was back in the 70's. We had no fear. However, one aspect of being able to walk in our destiny is that we are to learn from our mistakes; obviously, I did not. Here I was some three years later, in the car with a stranger, but as the "nice" man screamed for me to shut up, somehow this time, his voice pierced so deeply within me that I knew I was done with hitchhiking...forever.

How many times has your "mistake" become a habit? You got away with "it" the first time, and then again, and again. Yes, there are warning signs, and at some point you know you should let it go...that you should not do "it" again. You know the consequences could be devastating. You know this. You know in your spirit that eventually you will run out of chances. For some people, the consequences will be costly; they will change their lives forever, but they do it just one more time. They gamble with their God-given destiny just one more time. For some, your "IT" is playing in your mind right now. You know exactly what your "it" is and you know exactly how that "it" can swallow up your destiny. I am here to tell you to just stop. Acknowledge the seriousness of your ways. **Pick up your journal and write about your "IT." What are the consequences of continuing to do the thing that you know is wrong? List the people who will be hurt or disappointed.** Will you be embarrassed if you are exposed? Will you lose money? Will you lose someone's trust? Write about "IT."

Look at your "IT" on paper and all of the harmful possibilities that you might bring about. Is IT worth it?

My life could have ended that day. My son could have grown up without his mother. My daughter would not even exist. My parents could have been heartbroken by the loss of their child. My brother could have been burdened with the misfortune of growing up without his big sister. But God gave me another chance through a stranger and since that day, I have not hitchhiked. I recognized the enemy's intent behind that wayward thinking, but I also recognized God's hand in that incident.

You must see the "it" for what it really is, that thing that the enemy will use to influence you to go down a path that you know is wrong. For the children of Israel, it was their disobedience, so many died, not getting into the promise land. Moses attitude prevented him from making it in. For Samson it was Delilah. For Saul, it was himself. In 1

Kings, a lion killed a man because he did not obey the word of the Lord. For him it was his disobedience. What is “It” for you?

Prayer: Father, I thank you that you have given me free will. I choose to acknowledge your hand on my life and recognize any disobedience on my part. I repent, and I choose to let it go. I will seek you first and your kingdom and your righteousness. I choose to lean not to my own understanding and my own will. I choose to seek you in all things. I ask you to direct my path as I acknowledge you as Lord of my life. Thank you, Lord for your direction over my life.

Chapter 5

Stop talking, Sweetie!

I watched him grip that over-sized, over packed footlocker with his one good hand. With the strength of two strong wrestlers, he yanked it up in the air just a few inches from the floor. Dragging his bad leg, and holding his bad arm in its usual L-shaped position, he began his journey down the stairs. They were rugged; they were many; they were not friendly to disabilities, and there was no elevator. Tackling the stairs...that was the final piece, the last chapter.

That old footlocker would be the last to be stuffed into my daddy's broken down Buick. He loved those cars and never even considered getting any other model, and every car was always old and run down.

Arms loaded with the last three years of my life, I closed the door and stared out the passenger side window. Daddy sat in the driver's seat, with his left leg still on the pavement. He had his own technique, his own strategy for getting that leg into the car. Reaching over his own lap with his good hand, he grabbed the leg, picking it up off the ground and forcing it into position. Now settled, he cranked the old Buick, threw it in gear, and drove slowly out of the parking lot.

I didn't look back as we drove away. Tears filled my eyes, fiercely spilling over my eyelids, burning my cheeks as they settled under my chin. I was now a drop-out—the first in my family to go to college, the first to get a scholarship, the first to receive financial aid, the first to make the Dean's list, and now the first to be a dropout. As we rode along the country highway in uncomfortable silence, my heart was full. The pain seemed almost deadly. The fear was overwhelming and the shame was unbearable. I was so disappointed in myself; there were just no words.

About an hour into the trip, my daddy broke the silence. "Kiddo," he said, in his most gentle voice.

Kiddo was his sweet name for me. And my brother was Bo. "Kiddo, You ain't the first, and you sho' won't be the last."

At that moment, I broke down. Sobbing uncontrollably, I sank deeper into the cushion of the seat. I folded into a fetal position and wept. "He knows," I said to myself. "Oh Lord, my daddy knows."

He quickly reached over to touch my hand, and quickly put his hand back on the wheel. "Kiddo, you gone be the president of the United States one day." And then he was silent, for the rest of the trip.

I still can't get over the shock that my daddy drove nearly 300 miles by himself to come get me. He never did that because of the stroke, because his good hand couldn't handle driving long distances. My brother told me he was coming, but Daddy came alone.

Did my daddy know that I would be too ashamed to face anyone else— that I was so depressed that I had wished for death? Did he know that my department head told me and the other English majors that I would never amount to anything?

Did he know I would need to hear his silly, habitual declaration over me—that I would be the president one day or that today his words would give me the solace and hope that I needed? I often think of that day—the day I had to come to terms with the fact that I was pregnant, embarrassed and frightened beyond measure.

I had no idea through the pain that what was meant for bad would actually work for my good. Often, we fall for the lie that a major distraction will definitely get us off track forever. But when we are fighting for our destiny, fighting for our dreams, it is the enemy's job to use any and everything against us, and one weapon is talk.

The enemy would have us think in our mess-ups and wrong decision making, that everyone is talking about us. Everyone is making fun of us. Everyone is saying, "I knew it. I knew she would never amount to anything." Yes, that is what my department head said about me to my face and to my classmates.

Thank God for my daddy and my other family members who stood by me, who did everything they could to get me back on track. There were others who said negative things. They said things like, "But you were an A student. I can't believe you got pregnant."

Wait. I have never figured that one out. A's, sex. A's, sex. How are they connected? Still, for quite some time, I was depressed, especially with hearing all of the things that people said about me and to me.

I'll never forget the day my grandmother told me to go comb my hair. She said, "You dragging around here looking all crazy, but you just might feel better if you go comb that hair! Just cause you fall in da' mud puddle don't mean you got to wallow in it!"

What! The mud puddle? What was she saying? What did she mean? Don't wallow in it? What was I supposed to do? I had messed up my life, but here she was telling me to do something, to stop feeling sorry for myself, to stop making excuses for staying in my mess. After all, this was not just my life anymore, she said. "You having a baby."

Finally, I started to understand. She was telling me to do something. She was telling me to get with the plan, the plan that I had since I was a child. I could be the teacher that I was going to school to be. My daddy said I could rise above this. He said I wasn't the first to have a baby out of wedlock and that I would not be the last. I was getting it. I was. My teacher said I wouldn't amount to anything, but my daddy said I would, and so I believed me daddy.

Years later I understand. Back then, I didn't realize that I needed to simply stop "hearing" the negative talk. I needed to simply say, "Stop talking to me," if not aloud, then to myself as I separated myself from the negative words that were being spoken over me. I started to get my right thinking back. I started to feel like I could carry on with what I was destined to do. But I had to have a plan.

I was excited, and in my quest for direction and destiny-seeking strategies, I made another mistake. I started sharing my plans and dreams with people. I started talking about my plans to go back to school, to get that degree, and to teach on a college level one day. I was so naïve. I now know that not only should I have said to certain people, "Stop talking, Sweetie," but I should have said that to myself. "Stop talking, Linda!"

Some "friends" literally reminded me that I now had a baby to care for and that I should focus on getting a job at the bank or factory in my hometown so I could handle the responsibility of taking care of my illegitimate child. They told me to forget about going back to college to finish my last year. "It's too late for that," one "friend" said to me.

One person whom I saw as a mentor told me that instead of trying to go back to college, I needed to focus on seeking forgiveness from the Lord for having a child out of wedlock. Even though I had not confessed salvation when I became pregnant, she said I needed to seek forgiveness anyway. With that one, I was overwhelmingly confused. My son was two years old when I actually asked the Lord into my heart. I thought I was forgiven that night when I prayed the "Sinners' Prayer."

However, according to my spiritual mentor, that was not the case. "There are some sins that we can just ask for forgiveness for," she said.

"But there are others that we will just have hold by the hand as we walk down the street, as we go on with our lives. Those sins are ever before us," she explained. But even as a young Christian, that made no sense to me, yet I spent many, many days and nights at the altar, asking God for forgiveness.

One day a brother in Christ pulled me aside and told me to listen to his recording.

I sat there, almost in shock as he told me that I did not need to do what I was doing. "Forgive me, Lord," I heard my voice saying on the recording. "Forgive me, Lord."

He told me that the Lord had already forgiven me for my sins, and that I needed to chill out and stop going to the altar at every single altar call.

"My goodness," he said. "You make me tired just listening to that." He went on to explain that forgiveness was real.

I told him about my instructions and the godly wisdom that my mentor imparted to me. I was careful not to call her name, but my brother told me that there comes a time when I have to realize that I can't share my heart with everybody. But I knew that person's status is in the church. She had said those things. Then he said, "And what does the Word say?"

You see knowing when to share and with whom to share is so very important when you are on your road to your future. I tell people all the time not to share their dreams with people who don't believe in their dreams. I am saying to you don't share your vision with someone of less vision. Don't share your plans with someone who doesn't see your plans coming to pass.

Not long ago, a person told me that her friend is constantly talking down to her. She said every time she has an idea or implements changes in her business strategy, her friend calls her up to tell her what is wrong with everything that she is doing. She said her friend makes her feel like she can't do anything right.

I looked at her and asked, "Why do you tell her your business. You need to stop talking."

Happy People, listen to me. Stop talking to the wrong people. Stop telling your business to people who are not for you.

These are your plans. This is your destiny. This is your purpose—the one that God has for you. This is your journey. Why continue to share with someone who is obviously not for you.

Stop talking, Sweetie. Enough is enough!

It doesn't matter who that person is—your friend from childhood, your sister, your brother, your mom, your dad, your co-worker. Get it into your head and heart. That is not your "person." Find your person, that friend who will tell you that you can make it, who will say, "I am praying for you." Find your person, and in the meantime, stop talking. Maybe for the time being, your person is God.

I have to say that sometimes, people don't mean to do you harm. Sometimes, though rarely, they really think they are helping you. I will never forget when I told my friend back in 1999 that I was filing for a divorce. My husband had threatened to kill me, and in the midst of his drugging, I was afraid that he might be serious. Much of my marriage had been spent with my dodging drug dealers, protecting my children from "drive-by my house" shootings, and coming home to an emptied house—no furniture, no appliances, no nothing—all sold for drugs. Those things I had dealt with over and over, but my husband had never threatened to kill me, and in his right mind, he would never hurt me or anyone else, for that matter. When I told my friend that I was getting a divorce, she cried. She believed in us. "I just don't believe God told you to divorce him," she said through her tears. I remember putting my arms around her, consoling her.

"Don't cry, "I said. "He told me, so don't worry about it. You don't have to believe it."

That was pretty much the reaction of many people. It bothered me that it didn't seem to matter to them that he said he would kill me. But here is the real problem. Why did I continue to talk about it? Why was I telling these people my plans? It finally hit me that I needed to stop talking. I had peace about this. My children in all of their struggles had peace about it. I just needed to stop talking about it.

Seriously, I needed someone to simply say, "Stop talking, Sweetie." **Yes, it is time to write your list. In your journal, make two simple columns—** My People and Not My People. You know by now who should be in each column, and you know what you need to do. There's nothing else to be said here. This is your destiny at stake. **Write the list**. **Accept** it for what it is and **move on.** Just do it.

Somewhere down through the years, I learned when to talk and when to be quiet. I learned to recognize my cheerleaders and discern my enemies. I also learned another important aspect about having cheerleaders to speak wisdom into my life. It is not always about my need for encouragement or my need for loving correction. You see, it is not always about me. I am blessed to have cheerleaders who are for me, who speak over me, who help to change my atmosphere by just saying, "This is so good." Sometimes, it's about nurturing that relationship.

So in getting wisdom, we must get an understanding as well. We must understand that our cheerleader will sometimes NEED a cheerleader, too. Make sure your every phone call is not about your own need. Make sure you take some time to check on your cheerleader's needs, things like does you cheerleader need an encouraging word? Does your cheerleader need a hug like you sometimes do? Just maybe your cheerleader needs to hear you say, "I think you did a good job. Don't listen to that criticism." Do you need to say to your person, "Stop talking, Sweetie," because you realize your person is talking to enemies? Your person speaks life. Sometimes, you need to do the same. And whatever you do, let kindness be on your lips at all times.

Often, we have a tendency to say hurtful things to those who are closest to us, especially if our cheerleaders are relatives. Don't be guilty of hurting your person, the one person who will always be by your side, the one person who has always had your back. If your cheerleaders are your parents, honor them always. No matter who your cheerleaders are—maybe a friend from childhood, or perhaps a sibling, a spouse, mom, dad, even if you disagree with them, you should always watch your tone and watch your words. Don't take their forgiveness for granted. You have heard the saying, "You don't miss the water until the well runs dry." I say, "You don't miss your cheerleaders until they are no longer cheering."

Prayer: Lord help me to see and appreciate my blessings, in your name.

Chapter 6

Did that just happen?

The road seemed dreary, lonely, long, never ending. The curves and hills multiplied as I drove along the paths that often wound quickly and without warning.

As night began to engulf me, I fought back the tears.

"God did not give me the spirit of fear, but of love, peace, and a sound mind."

I had made this trip so many times from Union, Mississippi to Bradenton, Florida.

Why did I get off the regular road this time?

I reminded myself that I had the power to take my thoughts captive, but the darkness was closing in, and I began to fall apart on the inside. My hands were sweaty, and my heart beat so loudly that I could hear it pounding fiercely through my chest.

Still, I kept my eyes on the beaten path, the bumpy, graveled road that had no beginning and obviously no ending. What in the world would I do?

Looking at the gas gauge, I could clearly see that I was running out of time and gas. I was not quite on empty, but the tiny needle was quickly moving downward.

By now, darkness had reached me, and there were no lights or signs of civilization. Why had I taken this road? The map showed to be a short-cut. Never mind the gravel. Never mind the one-way ruts. Never mind the long, deserted path.

Funny how the map never showed any indication of these three very important aspects of this short-cut. I knew I couldn't turn around. I didn't have the gas. Plus, I didn't know which way to go even if I did. I was obviously lost, and I was scared.

It felt like I had been driving for hours. Out of nowhere, I saw the dim lights. Getting closer, I could see that it was a gas station, out in the middle of nowhere, and it seemed to just appear. But by now, though, it was after 1 a.m. "Lord, let it be open."

I drove up to the pump, slowly and deliberately, looking around into the darkness, trying desperately to be aware of my surroundings. Surroundings? There were no surroundings—just darkness, barrenness, and a dim light shining in a run-down building. As I neared the pumps, my doom became even more certain. Shining my brights directly on the pumps, I could see orange, plastic bags covering the hoses, tightly secured, wrapped with wide, black, duct tape. Yes, this place, whatever it was, was closed.

Taking a deep breath, I remained calm. "Lord, I thank you," I said aloud, so I could hear myself. "Whatever your plan is, I know you have one. I know you have this. So I praise you. I glorify you. I exalt your Holy name, and I declare it done."

My mind went back to a day that I was reading Psalm 100. "Serve the LORD with gladness: *come before* his *presence with singing*. Know ye that the LORD he is God: it is he that hath made us, and not we ourselves." As I read the scripture, I heard a still voice say, "Read it, again." I started to read, and what I heard changed my life. "Serve the LORD with gladness: *come before* his *presence with singing*. Come before you feel his presence. Come before you see a change. Come before the fight is over. Come before all of these things with singing. Know ye that the LORD he is God: it is he that hath made us, and not we ourselves."

"My Lord," I said as I sat in the darkness. "You WILL make a way out of no way. I thank you." And then I was silent. I would not cry. I had just prayed. I had been praying all along, so I had to call things that were not as though they were.

This was my perfect opportunity to practice what I preached. "When you are believing God, you have to believe God," I always said. "You have to faith it til you make it. You have to talk it til you walk it. You have to act it til you fact it. You have to believe it til you see it."

I took another deep breath, holding it in for a while, and slowly letting it out.

I had to get my bearings. I had to be still. Just as I started to put the car in "drive," I heard a soft tap on the window. I cannot begin to describe the chill that went through me at that moment. Standing there with a small flashlight, an old man waited for me to roll down my window. I had not seen his light coming toward me. Why? With little time to think, I slowly cracked the window.

My hands were trembling as I leaned in to get a better view. I could see the wrinkles in his face, especially on his forehead. He was a Caucasian man, a very old man.

Even in the darkness, the tiny lines on his face painted a story of his life and old age. My mind quickly filled with questions. Where did he come from? Why hadn't I seen him coming with the flashlight? It was so strange—scary, just plain ol' weird.

"There's a filling station about 15 miles down the road," he said. His voice was soft, almost gentle, but it was still a strong voice. "I ain't a station. I used to be but I closed down a long time ago. Nobody comes this way, you know. I just came out to get some old tools, and just sat down to rest a while. What 'chu doing out here?"

I sat there staring at him, speechless, motionless, still in shock at his appearance, only to hear him say that he had no gas. I knew I wouldn't make it 15 miles down the road. My little 79 Toyota got good gas mileage, but not 15 more miles. I knew it.

Evidently, the look on my face said so, too. And as he continued to talk, I just stared at him, dumb-founded.

"You don't think you can make it, do you? Well, open up your tank. I gotta can of gasoline in the back of my truck.

I'll pour it in your tank. You'll be al'right."

Still motionless, still speechless, I reached under my steering wheel and pushed the hatch. I could hear him doing something to my car, bumping, moving, jiggling something, but I couldn't see what he was doing. I kept trying to see, and I kept my lights on, just for good measure. Then as fast as he appeared, he tapped my window again and said, "That oughta get you there."

Oh my gosh! My heart was so full. I immediately reached over to get some money from my purse, then turned to give it to him through the cracked window and to thank him. I had looked away for only a minute to get the money, but in that moment, there was no flashlight and no light from the building. Just darkness. He was gone.

Through many trials and tribulations, I have thought about that trip to Florida. God came through for me that night in nowhere land. I cannot explain what happened to me that night. It makes no sense, but those things have happened to me so many times.

I remember the day before I graduated with my bachelor's degree. It was back in the day, before computers and data bases. Graduating students were always nervous because the College was known for pulling people out of the lines during the graduation line-up.

Office clerks often worked late on Friday nights and very early on Saturday mornings, right on through the graduation ceremony, looking for people who were missing an hour or two, and were, therefore, not eligible to walk across the stage. With friends and family there, each graduate was a basket case, and I was no different.

But on this day, I was in the administration building taking care of one last piece of business before the next day ceremony. The place was packed. People were shoulder to shoulder, trying for the last time to get a final clearance before graduation the next day. The noise factor was overwhelming, and people were scrambling around, forging their paths, able to take only one or two small steps at a time.

Finally, after two hours, I squeezed my way to the desk and proudly gave the lady my name. "I'm Linda Mason," I said. "I came to pick up my honor's cord." I had dropped out of school twice, but in the midst of the drama, having a baby, being on welfare and food stamps, dropping out, I maintained a 3.9 GPA. I had even been homeless for a short time, but my friend let me sleep in her car on campus. She could have been expelled if I were caught sleeping in her dorm room. But now, all of those memories seemed null and void. I was about to graduate, in less than 24 hours and with honors!

The lady left the counter, disappearing into another room, then quickly reappeared with a shiny, golden, yellow cord. It was so beautiful, and it belonged to me!

"That will be five dollars," she said.

What? Five dollars? But no one told me that I would have to pay for my cord. I had earned it, paid for it with blood, sweat, tears, and long walks to campus when I didn't have a dime for a bus transfer. Five dollars! I didn't have five dollars! I didn't even have five cents.

"But I don't have five dollars," I said, through the tears that were now creeping over my eyelids. “Please. I don’t have any money. I paid my graduation fee. I don’t have five dollars.”

“Then you won’t get the cord,” she snapped, ready to move on to the next person. “It costs five dollars.”

People were pushing and reaching, making demands and talking loudly. It was chaotic, but I stayed through the chaos for over two hours, so excited to get my cord. This woman was so rude. She was cold and determined to keep the cord that had my name on it. I could see that she just didn’t care.

Suddenly, without notice, I heard a loud bang, as an aged, white-haired, black man slammed his fist upon the counter.

It startled me and shook the woman who had my cord in her hand. She stood frozen, starring at the old man, as did I. His white hair was thick, nappy, and looked like a white afro. The tiny lines of wrinkles under his eyes looked like a child's drawing of tree branches, spread far and wide. His dark, dry skin seemed to draw us into his world. And we were silent.

Surely he was nearing a hundred years old. His eyes were glued on the woman, and he never, no not once, looked at me. He was not there just a minute before, and it took people hours to get even close to the front, yet here he was at the desk!

"Give this baby her honor's cord," he said sternly and loudly, planting a five dollar bill on the desk.

The lady, without thinking, silently and quickly, shoved the cord toward me, and as I turned to thank the Centurion, he was gone. The two of us stood there, making eye-contact, confused, knowing we were thinking the same things.

Where did he come from? Where did he go so quickly? Did anyone else see him? Did they hear him? Slowly, she reached for the money as I quickly reached for my cord, and without even waiting for a receipt, I left.

As you move along your journey trying to follow your pathway toward your destiny, trying to fulfill your purpose in different stages of your life, you can be sure of one thing. As God's child, you can know without a doubt, that he has your back. Your age does not matter. Whether you are 2, 22, or 92, if you are still alive on this earth, you have a purpose to fulfill. You can be sure that He will do what the elderly Christians used to sing about. He will make a way out of no way.

Many times, on the road, you will find that you don't know what to do. You don't see a way out, but I guarantee you that when you deliberately stop to think about your other times of need, you will remember how God came through for you. Listen to me. If he did it once, he will do it again. He has made promises in the Word. He promises to never leave you or forsake you. He will do what he says that he will do.

You must hold on to your dreams, for he promises to bless your plans. If it involves financial woes, he said he will supply your needs. Do you need protection? He is your refuge, your help in a time of trouble. Is the enemy trying to take you out? God will make your enemy your footstool. Is it your health? The word says you are already healed. Even sleeping—He promises to give you peaceful sleep at night and to give you a perfect peace that you can't even understand.

My former pastor once said, "You can reach heaven and still not reach your destiny." Think about that—reach heaven, but not your destiny here on earth.

There are so many things that hinder us from walking in our call—our destiny. It may be a particular position in the church, a particular call that's not church related—your job, your education, your marriage partner, your marriage, your everyday decision making—whatever. For many, it is wrong thinking. Some fail to remember that in this life, we will all have challenges, but God will deliver us out of the hand of the enemy. He has done it before, and he will do it again. The word says his promises are sure. There is a saying that goes something like, "If you fail to believe in something, you will fall for anything." Of course, that is not exactly right, as I seem to be challenged when it comes to remembering clichés. But you get the idea, right? You have to make a decision to trust God.

I know Christians who are always wishy washy. Every time there's a storm, they let it sidetrack them instead of remembering that He led them to the other side during the last storm. I almost let depression steal my destiny. When I finally made the decision to fight, there were days when I literally picked my legs up and put them on the floor. I would yell, "Legs! You will walk!"

My tendency was to stay in bed and sleep. I would go to work and church, smile, fake, and do my job and church duties well. As soon as the work day or the church service was over, I was in bed, refusing to face the life that I was forced to live, through no fault of my own. Of course, you caught that, right?

It was not my fault. It was everybody else's fault. Whatever. The bottom line was I had two children who depended on me. I had to decide to make a change, to trust God with my destiny. After all, he had plans for me, to give me good things and not bad things, to give me peace and not calamity, to bring me to an expected end.

Here's the deal though. I seriously believe that we play a part in our Jeremiah 29:11—to bring us to an expected end. I believe we must expect the end to line up with the word of God. I believe we must look at the last part of that scripture as our part in helping to bring the scripture to fruition. We must expect and declare greatness. We are kings and queens. Our daddy is rich in houses and lands. He says he will supply our needs according to his riches in glory. He owns glory. He owns the land. He owns us. And if he brought us through one trial, big, little, small, even insignificant to others, He will do it again. **What are your dreams? Write them in your journal and be sure to date the page. What are you doing right now that will help you fulfill your dream? If you have goals, they can substitute for dreams, but at any rate, write your dreams down. Habakkuk 2:2 tells you to write your vision and keep it before you.**

Write about your dreams each day and be faithful to mark accomplishments off your list and **careful to give God the praise for every accomplishment**.

Indecision is just as serious as wrong thinking. They both become strongholds. Scripture calls that double-minded. Whichever is the case, the end result is disobedience, and disobedience definitely holds us back from our destiny. Wrong thinking leads to having a wrong perception of life. That is a hindrance. When my daughter was only 6 years old, she came home from school one day and asked me how people can say they are having a bad day at 8:00 in the morning. "The day just started," she said. She went on to say, "If it has not been a full day, how can people say it's a bad day? It's not really a day, yet," she said.

What wisdom for a 6-year-old. She was talking about her young classmates. No doubt, they had heard their parents or other adults declare bad days, so they were following suit. My daughter is a married woman now, but through the years I have thought of her 6-year-old perspective on bad days. Often today, when I walk into my classroom, I say,

"Good morning, Happy People! It's a great day to have a great day!" Because you know what? It really is. And whatever negative is going on in my life at 8:00 in the morning, I make a conscious decision to declare that it will NOT dictate my entire day. God always comes to my rescue, and if he did it time and time again, He will do it again.

Sometimes we don't stop to think about how our lack of trust in God can affect our destiny and even those whose lives we touch. I remember when I was only 9 years old and had to come to terms with death among a family that was close to me.

My childhood best friend was with her aunt one night, along with seven other people. In addition, her aunt was pregnant. The story that I heard was that a young man had just broken up with his girlfriend and made the decision to end his life. I overheard the adults saying he decided to kill himself by driving on the wrong side of the road because his life was no longer worth living. Perhaps that was true for him, but he made a decision that affected the lives of eight other people. My friend's aunt was killed, along with one of her daughters and her unborn child as well. Another daughter was seriously injured and was in a body cast for a very long time. My best friend was injured and even now, 53 years later, she has pins in her arm to show for it.

Her aunt's two, small sons were in the car and were both injured and there was another passenger as well. The young man who orchestrated the accident, died in the crash, forfeiting his destiny, but he took several destinies with him. He also caused major changes in the lives of those who survived.

Imagine what life could have been like for the kids who lost their mom if this young man had decided to trust God to see him through. Imagine what could have happened if he had said, "God has seen me through before, and He will do it again."

Scripture says our steps, the steps of the righteous, are ordered of the Lord. It doesn't say he makes us take those steps. He orders them, sets them up. He blesses our plans, but it's up to us to nurture those steps and the blessings he puts before us.

He can lead us to a job and even open doors to place us on the job, but he won't make us do the job so we can keep it. He can put two people together in a marriage, give them their dream mates, but he won't make them do what it takes to stay married. He can give us words of prophesy and promises, but we have to realize that prophesies and promises are conditional.

Indeed, Jeremiah 29:11 does say he has a plan for our destiny to bring us good things and not bad things; he has plans to bring us to an expected end, but it is up to us to expect the right things and to do the right things to take us to that destined end. We have to realize that the storms of life will come, but they come and yes, they go. Experience has taught me that storms have no respect of person.

They come when life is going well, and often they catch us off guard. They come when things are not going well, adding to the "When it rains, it pours," syndrome. But if we let him, Jesus will be in the midst of the storm with us. He will give us directions, strength and wisdom if we ask. And sometimes, even when we forget to ask, he will do what he does best—keep his word. He will rescue us not once, not twice but as many times as we need him too. He will not forsake us. If he led us through the storm before, he will do it again. We have to realize that he will lead us to our destiny if we listen to him and obey him; if we keep the faith, watch our words, actions, and expectations, we can walk in our destiny; we can see prophecies and promises fulfilled in our lives, and we can enjoy the journey.

Prayer: Lord, I acknowledge you in all of my ways. Thank you for leading me, for always being there for me. I love you, Lord.

Chapter 7

Why you on that side?

It was 3:37 in the morning. Streets were dark, silent and deserted, but I knew it was my car. Gunning the motor, I sped up, driving the speedometer up to an unlawful speed. I was getting closer, but not close enough. I had to catch them before they purposely got me off course.

I noticed the darkness getting even darker, realizing there were now no street lights. What were they doing? Where were they going? The silence made the journey feel cold and dangerous, just the way it actually was in reality.

Abruptly, the driver stopped the car in the middle of nowhere. Complete blackness enveloped me, except for the lights from my car that the crook was driving and the lights from my son's car that I was driving. I could see three more people in my car. "Four on one. Not good," I thought.

Quickly jumping out of my car, a wicked looking man ran angrily toward me. But with just as much anger and fury, I jumped out of my son's car, meeting him head on.

"Why you following me," the man yelled. His voice was impatient and obviously full of rage.

And though fear and common sense should have gripped me, instead I ran toward him, like David confronting Goliath. And like David, I had a mission, and being afraid was not part of it.

"That's my car!" I screamed, feeling the veins in my neck expanding. Enough is enough, I thought to myself. This 6 foot giant did not scare me, and his tactics definitely did not impress me.

"Get your buddies out of my car, and do it now!"

Within seconds, we were toe to toe and head to chest, since I was a mere 5'4" compared to this villain. "Give me my car!"

"You know yo' o' man gave us this car. You know what the deal is!"

"I don't care! Give me my car now, or...."

"Or what?" he said looking down at me, cutting me off in mid-sentence. Using a few choice words, he stepped closer and looked me in the eye.

I could see the evil in his eyes, even in the pitch blackness.

"Or what, Miss? Woman, I will kill you, right now!"

Suddenly, before I even had a chance to lose my courage, he looked up into the darkness of the sky and simply froze. Standing there, as fear came over him, he put his hands over his face as if to protect it from a bright light or a massive blow.

"Get away from me!" he yelled, staring upward. "Get away!" Turning his back to me, right then and there, he ran, disappearing into the darkness.

Immediately, another passenger sprang from the car, no doubt another drug dealer cause birds of a feather flock together. He came at me with full speed but he, too, stopped in his tracks just a few inches from me. "What tha" he began, but quickly covered his face, turned from me and ran into the darkness.

This same scene would play out twice more as each passenger jumped from the car to take the reign of putting me in my place. Each one stopped, looked into the sky, covered his face, and bailed.

I stood there, stunned, alone in the black of night, as a calmness overwhelmed me. It was if someone literally embraced me and held me until my body stopped shaking. For the first time, I felt the tears begin to spill over my lids, as I realized what had just happened. "Thank you, Lord, for your angel. It must have been mighty big."

I often think back to that night and each time, I thank God for protecting me, for guiding me out of that darken place, and for showing me how to get back the next day to get my son's car. You see, I left it there that night because I knew the drug dealers might have another key to my car.

Many times I tell that story when I want to talk about miracles, how God sent his supernatural power to protect me and save me from possible death. But that's not why I am telling this story this time. I am telling it to make a more relevant point at this moment. You see, it was crazy of me to try to take the law into my own hands. I was not supposed to be acting like a trained cop. As amazing as that story is, the truth is I was out of my lane and that night, being on the wrong side of the road could have cost me my purpose in life. More specifically, it could have cost me my life.

I attended a Jazz concert not long ago. One of the performers, Joe, came on stage with a guitar in hand and began to play. He plays the piano, so I had never heard him on the guitar. He was amazing, but then the concert guitarist came out, took the instrument, and began to play. He was even better. As the guitarist played, Joe got on the drums and joined in. My goodness. He played the drums, too. He was amazing, but then the concert drummer came out and took over the drums. He was even better. As the drummer and guitarist continued to play, Joe walked over and picked up the saxophone and began to play. This man was good! He played that saxophone like a pro. He was amazing, but then the concert saxophonist came out on stage, took the instrument and began to play. He was even better.

Finally Joe walked over to the keyboard and joined in with the rest of the band. The music was outstanding, and Joe could make the keyboard talk. He could make it get up and go clean your house. He was just good! Everyone stood up, moving to the beat of the music, marveling at the excellence of this performance. When the song ended, Joe went on to explain how he has the ability to play several instruments, "But," he said, "it's so much better when we all get on our own instrument. Isn't it so much better when we stay in our own lane?" he asked.

Happy People, as you tread through the journey of finding and following the road to your destiny, one of the most important things you can do is stay on your own path—not your neighbor's path, not your sister's path, not your co-worker's path, not even your spouse's path.

Many times, we stay in the desert for 40 years, circling, going backwards, losing direction because we jumped in someone's lane.

Just because your friend quit his job and started a business, it does not mean that is what you are supposed to do. Perhaps your friend spent his life-long savings and his business was successful in no time. But perhaps God has a different route for you. If you quit your job, your business just might go under.

Are you facing some issues right now? Are you thinking about getting involved, tangled up in something that is not part of the vision God has given you? Are you playing around with getting on the wrong side of the road just to keep up with your friends?

Figure it out. Being true to yourself, write down some things that are burdens that you should not be carrying. Let them go. Yes, you read correctly—burdens. It is hard to live your life in someone else's lane. It is tiring, unpredictable, and sometimes even dangerous.

Back in the day, I had a cousin who was well into his sixties before he ever learned to drive. We all lived in the country, where we had a narrow, graveled road leading to all of our houses. The road was just wide enough to be called a two-lane dirt road.

When we saw our new driver making his way down the road, we were very careful to give him the road courtesy that he needed. Folks, he was not the best driver. I don't know to this day how he got his license or who taught him to drive.

Surely none of the family members did it. But then the day came when he decided to teach his 60 something year-old wife to drive.

Let me tell you, this was a dangerous pair, so we all tried to just stay off the road when she was practicing. She was bad—really bad, so bad that our cousin noticed how nervous we were when he was giving her daily driving lessons.

Still, he often reassured us that we didn't need to worry.

"She be doing al'ight til she be gitting on the wrong side of da' road," he often said, explaining to us that was the hardest thing for her to learn.

I don't remember whether or not she finally learned to drive, but her husband's explanation for her lack of success has stayed with me—that her journey was going well until she got on the wrong side of the road. She was progressing until she got over in someone else's lane. Isn't that the case many times? Your life is going alright. You are living within your means. You are holding down that position at work and at church. You are doing you. But then for some ridiculous reason, you decide to do "her." She's buying a huge house, so you decide to buy a huge house, one you can't afford by the way. She bought a Benz, so you decide to buy a Benz, a car you can't afford. She is marrying a pastor, so you set out to do the same, and it just goes on and on. Perhaps all of these are things she has worked for. Maybe she planned for these things.

Perhaps, she used her 401K. I mean who knows how she was able to afford all of these new items. But see, that's not the point. That's her lane, or maybe it isn't. The bottom line though is it is not yours.

Maybe you were doing alright til you started getting on the wrong side of the road—til you got in her lane and left the path to your own journey. Why are you on that side? Whose destiny are you seeking?

Prayer: Thank you Lord for Jeremiah 29:11 that you have a plan for my life, and I ask you to guide my steps, Lord, that I will not get off track. I praise you, Lord. Thank you.

Chapter 8

That's not the way you roll!

It was a quiet morning. The usually busy street was deserted. Not a mouse was stirring, but there was one creature—a squirrel. It lay helplessly in the streets and I immediately thought of my friend who needed a squirrel for her class project. My three-year-old sat buckled in her car seat, watching and listening as I talked my way through my fear of the dead squirrel. It would be for a good cause, a good grade for my friend. My baby girl confirmed the same. "You can do it, Mommy. You can do it."

Ah, she had such confidence in her wimpy mom. That's what convinced me to do it. I spread a sheet of newspaper on the floor board of my old 67 Chevy. The big hump in the middle was between the squirrel and me. Plus, he was dead, not bloody at all, but dead. Obviously, the car that hit him did not drag him along. He was dead, but otherwise, in perfect condition.

"You can do it, Mommy," my baby said, as I wrapped the newspaper around the squirrel's tail and lifted him into the car onto the paper. "Yay for Mommy!"

Thank goodness, we were just one block from home. My friend would be so thankful for her science project.

As I got settled on the driver's side and started to put the car in gear, the dead squirrel suddenly began moving and literally stood up and stared at me. In shock, I immediately jumped out of the car, noticing still that the streets were empty.

I could hear my poor little cheer-leader screaming, "Don't leave me, Mommy! Don't leave me!"

I mean who does that? Who leaves the little one in the back seat to run from the staggering squirrel? I watched through the window as he fell over, but this time, he fell onto the hump in the car. Oh my lands! He would be right next to me, but he was still again.

Meanwhile, my baby was yelling, "Mommy!" Poor baby.

Mommy was thinking. That's right. She was thinking. Finally, I eased my body into the front seat and drove with madness around the block and into our driveway. I quickly unbuckled my little one, opened the front passenger side door, ran inside and waited.

My daughter and I pinned our eyes to the window as we waited for the now obviously NOT dead squirrel to get out of the car. Hours passed as we waited for him to get out. He never did. I can't remember how the story ended or who even got the squirrel out of the car. I just know I made the mistake of assuming he was dead, and y'all, he was not.

Often that is how the enemy gets us off track, through assumptions. No one told me the squirrel was dead. I made that assumption. It's a funny story now, one that didn't cost me a major setback, but what I went through was self-inflicted, all because I didn't know the real truth; I assumed that I did.

When I realized that squirrel was alive, my instinct was to give up on helping my friend with the assignment. And even in my fear, my baby girl continued to cheer me on. She was stubborn like that. Giving up was not in her DNA. Even though she was only three, that just wasn't the way she rolled.

I remember the night that I literally gave up. I had been doing so much better with the depression and with my wrecked life. I assumed I was okay, but I was not. That night, I lost the desire to fight. Curling down into a fetal position, I felt the darkness sinking in. Tears flooded my eyes and fiercely rolled down my cheeks and onto my neck. I felt a tightness in my chest, like something heavy was pressing against it. “It’s too much,” I thought to myself. “It’s too much.” It seemed as if I was no longer breathing, and why should I try? It was better this way. Someone would find me in the morning. I would die a natural death, depressed and alone.

In the lowest of times and in the worst of times, somewhere on your journey, you might feel as if there is no way out. Depression might take over and thoughts might try to trick you into thinking that everyone will be better off without you. But as God’s child, you have an advocate who will fight for you, who will provide a way out. For me, my 15-year-old son came home early from a ballgame. He said he felt like he was supposed to. God was looking out for me, and he did it through my son. Seeing me helpless and almost breathless in the chair, he immediately began praising God for my deliverance. I remember him screaming, "Devil! You will not take my mama. She will live and not die." God sent him home early to sing praises and to rescue his mama.

Sometimes on your journey, you may experience the lowest of the lows. That's when you have to "get it" that life is sometimes just hard. I remember the times when things were going okay, and then something unexpected would happen. That's life, though. Maybe you lost a loved one and you don't understand why. Maybe you lost your dream job, or your dream home, and you don't understand why. Maybe the depression is getting worse instead of better, and you don't understand why. Maybe your best friend since childhood turned out NOT to be your best friend after all, and the pain seems unbearable.

And to make it worse, you don't understand why. Through it all, God will give you the strength to keep going. You can't give up because that's just not the way you are supposed to roll. You must be persistent and be obedient in your pursuit of fulfilling your purpose. This is your life that you are fighting for. Your destiny will affect many other people as well. Just because there is a delay in getting something that you feel like you must have now, it doesn't mean it's God's denial. It just might not be the right timing. I always say "God, until you tell me no, I am going to believe it's a yes." Expect your deliverance. Expect your sudden rescue. It is on the way. You must make up your mind that no matter what, you will reach your destiny. You will have everything that God has for you.

Find scriptures to back it up. **In your journal, write them down. Write words of** affirmation. **Read the scriptures and affirmations and shout them out loud**. **Read them daily**. You need to hear what you have said about yourself and your situation. Then on another page, **go back in time and list some times when you felt low, but somehow you survived.**

If it happened then, it will happen again. **Renew your mind and spirit with the Word of God**. Giving up? That's just not the way you roll. The problem may be big, but your God is bigger. Talk to God about it, and until

He gives you a new word, **stand on the one that He gave you in the past**.

Prayer: Thank you Lord that your word says that I can do all things through you. I am more than a conqueror, for I am your child. I have your mind. I have your wisdom. I have your direction. I will not give up.

Chapter 9

It's your season!

Now, moving forward, it is time to celebrate. The woman at the well said to Jesus, "Sir, give me this water so I will thirst no more." Before she makes this statement though, her thoughts are not good. She wanted to know why in the world Jesus was there, and why would he even look at her, let alone talk to her. In her mind, this was not good.

There had to be more to this than what Jesus is saying. "Why are you here?" she wanted to know. Samaritans were known as heathens, characterized as idol worshippers and hypocrites. Often Jews said they never wanted to set eyes on a Samaritan. They would literally go to the other side of the street so they wouldn't have to be near a Samaritan. Can you imagine the pain on the inside of this woman? Whether it was her choice or her several husbands, she was NOT good with relationships. She couldn't get it right.

Do you think she might have experienced some shame, some depression, some embarrassment, some financial lack, and some endurance of maybe being the talk of the town?

But God was intentional. He was deliberate. And it is the same today. *God, Destiny, and a Glass of Wine* is intentional.

I believe if you are intentional in just following through on these simple, practical do's and don'ts, these tiny tidbits of wisdom, you are on your way to healing, and you are going to keep your healing.

God knew what the woman was going through—what she had been through. He knew how she was hurting.

He knew her strengths, her struggles with self-image, and her reputation.

Samaria was not considered part of the Holy Land. It was just an outcast, and Jesus didn't have to go that route. This route was out of his way, and would add days to his already three- day journey to get to his destination, but he went anyway because the woman at the well was worth it.

He saw something in her that no one else saw. Often, we don't see ourselves as Jesus does, as a conqueror, as an Esther, as a man of faith, a man of God, but God is intentional. He will cause someone to go out of his or her way, just to get to you, just to help you get back on the right track.

In II Corinthians 5:17, scripture says, "Therefore if anyone is in Christ, he is a new creature: old things are passed away; behold all things are become new." When that women went to that well, out of necessity and routine, she had no idea that her life would be changed forever, and when you read *God, Destiny, and a Glass of Wine,* I believe you put yourself in the same place, a place of change. But you must be willing to change.

Each year, I ask God for a word for the New Year. About two years ago, after praying for my word for quite some time, I heard him say, "Be filled." I was like, "Excuse me?" I knew he was leading me to fast for 21 days, but not from food in general—from desserts and candy bars. OMG! I don't cook sweet potato pies because I will eat the whole pie while it is still hot. I love pecan pie, and I will eat the whole pie in one sitting. I love chocolate covered pecans and peanuts. I sometimes ate three and four candy bars in a day. It was just pathetic. But

I finally agreed that's what I was supposed to do, starting, I thought, on the 11th of January. But then I heard in my spirit that I was to start "tomorrow," which was January 4th. I was like, "...but I have another week to eat my pies, and I have some candy that I didn't eat yet. There is half of a strawberry cake. I was going to eat that first, Lord!"

Finally, because the Lord insisted, I changed my thinking and started the next day, January 4th. That afternoon, my husband fell from a ladder, nearly 30 feet to the ground. He injured his rotator cuff, ripped his sleeves, cut his elbow, and his mouth, and hurt his leg, but he survived the fall. He fell just inches from a concrete slab, and he had a power saw in his hand. My friend's cousin fell only 10 feet and had a major head injury, a punctured lung, and a broken back. My husband did not. Of course, God protected him, but I believe changing my thinking and being obedient made a difference as well. I believe God was deliberate in starting the fast a week early.

But **"Be filled?** I still didn't get it. **Ephesians 3:19 says, "**know this love that surpasses knowledge—that you may be filled to the measure of all the fullness of God." How, Lord? How do I do this? I asked him.

He answered, "By changing your thinking." BE filled, he said with all of the fullness of God.

Now here is the clincher. To change where you are now, to get to the fullness of God, to get healed and keep your healing, you must talk Kingdom talk, you must think Kingdom thoughts, you must walk a Kingdom walk, you must act like a Kingdom heir, because your daddy has already promised you that he will supply your needs according to his riches in glory. He owns everything, and as his child, who is obeying his or her daddy, you have access to it if you simply believe it, really, really believe it.

"But how do I do this filled thing?" I again asked.

He said, "If you will purpose in your heart, to make it intentional to think on whatsoever things are true, whatsoever things are honest, whatsoever things are just, whatsoever things are pure, whatsoever things are lovely, whatsoever things are of good report, then there is no room for anything else— no room for worry, no room for envy, no room for bitterness, no room for unforgiveness, no room for doubt and unbelief, no room for illness, no room for poverty, no room for financial lack, no room for joblessness, no room for low self-esteem, no room for self-pity, no room for hurts from the past, no room for depression, no room for loneliness, no room for fear, no room for lying, no room for slacking, no room for criticizing, no room for complaining, no room for ungratefulness, no room for whining, no room for insecurity, no room, no room, no room."

To walk in victory, **Philippians 4: 8** is the key. When we fill our mouth and mind with things that are true, honest, just, pure, lovely, and of a good report, we will begin to meditate on his goodness, his mercy, his promises. When something tries to come in to make you worry, there is no room and so your response to the devil becomes automatic.

When the devil says you are going to lose everything you have, you WILL automatically think on things that are true! "Thank you, God that you are supplying all of my needs because YOU promised and I will stand on it. Your word is true!" And when the devil tries to come in and say, Cancer is going to take you out, you will automatically think on those things that of a good report: "God, thank you that your report says that I am healed! No matter how long it takes, no matter what the doctors say, I am standing on your word."

When the devil tries to say you will be laid off, or you can't do your job, or you will never find a job as good as what you had, don't entertain him. You must be deliberate. You know you have the power to take control of your thoughts. Scripture says so. Don't entertain that, not one minute because you know there is freedom in your thoughts and you have committed to always think on whatsoever things are true, whatsoever things are honest, whatsoever things are just, whatsoever things are pure, whatsoever things are lovely, whatsoever things are of a good report. You can automatically say, "Thank you, God that whatever I put my hand to will prosper."

You have to be filled with him by thinking what he has told you to think. You have to have the assurance that you can trust him. It won't happen overnight, but change can start right now, by changing your thought patterns. And if you read this book with intentional intention, change has already started.

I recently spoke at a women's revival. Many times I have told my husband what my message will be, but this time as I gathered my thoughts, I told him that I planned to talk about the woman at the well. Oh my goodness! He became so excited. He told me that he believed this story was full of symbolism and encouragement. The woman was in a dark place, he said, and visited the well when she could be there alone away from the other uppity women who criticized her and talked about her. The water in the well, he explained, represented new life for her, second chances and celebrations, and the whole story symbolized new beginnings.

This woman was given a second chance and with joy she celebrated by going into town and telling her story. She told about this man who knew her life's story, who gave her a drink that caused her to thirst no more. He gave her a living water that bubbled up on the inside. No, it did not change her past, but it did indeed change her future. And with this new knowledge, she celebrated a newness of life.

And so it is with you. In the *Bible*, wine symbolized transformation. You have been transformed even if it has been just a little at this time. As you look back on how far you have come, think about sitting in your favorite spot, maybe your favorite recliner, or your favorite chair on your back porch. Maybe your favorite spot is in the middle of your bed or in the middle of your backyard. It might be at your kitchen table or under your grandmother's big oak tree.

Wherever it is, sit back in your quiet place of reflection, and take a sip of your very favorite, fine wine to symbolize your transformation, to think about your new beginning, that path that leads to your destiny.

Or even better, take communion as you rededicate your thoughts and actions to fulfilling the purpose that God has for you. Take Jeremiah 29:11 even more seriously. Take God at his word.

He is not a man that he would lie. He is a promise keeper; He has a plan for you, to give you good and not evil, peace and not calamity. He has a plan to get you to your special place. He can enlarge your territory as you seek to keep his word and listen to his guidance over your life.

And if you are just not there yet with the glass of wine, that's okay. It's all good. You still need to celebrate! So grab your favorite drink—Coke, water, tea—whatever, and celebrate your amazing destiny and your miraculous transformation.

Celebrate the change that has happened, the change that is happening, and the change that is to come. Finally, in the process of going where you need to go, keep this in mind: If you run into a negative person on the way, KEEP RUNNING!"

Afterword

As we run this race toward our God-given destiny, let's be mindful of some things that can make the journey just a bit more enjoyable. Let's recap.

(1) **First, and most important, be quick to forgive**. Forgiveness brings life and good health. Forgiveness restores relationships and lengthens a person's life. Forgiveness is the key. Always go for it. Just do it! (2) **Recognize God-given opportunities** for what they are. Know that what you do on your journey will affect your life and the lives of others as well—for the good or for the bad. Choose "good." Just do it!

(3) **Don't repeat the same "IT" over and over**. If it doesn't speak life, let it go before you are forced to let it go. Stop "IT" while you are a head and not so far off track. You can do it. Just stop!

Just do it! (4) **Understand the principle of not telling your business to someone who is not your person**. And understand that sometimes you have to be bold enough to tell your enemy to just stop talking. You don't need to be rude, but you need to just do it!

(5) **Embrace God's rescue operations.** Yes, that miracle did just happen because you are marked by God. He will go to great extremes to protect you. He will rescue you, whether it is from a dangerous situation or a bad relationship. He is God. He will just do it!

(6) **Get in your lane and stay there**! You have no right to judge others or to try to do what they do. When you step into someone else's lane, you are saying you are not satisfied in the place where God has you at this time. Stay on your own course. Just do it!

(7) Remember that **you can't give up**. No matter what, you must keep going. As a child of God, giving up is never an option. You really can do all things through Christ who gives you strength. Giving up is just not the way you roll. Keep the faith. Just do it!

Perhaps you read *God, Destiny, and a Glass of Wine* in bits and pieces, a little at a time. Perhaps you picked up the book and read until you finished the entire piece. Maybe you read a chapter a week, implemented what you read, and then moved to the next chapter. You might have written down notes from each chapter as a reminder of what you needed to do.

But here's the bottom line. As you make changes in your life, as you overcome obstacles and master things that would have normally brought you to defeat, your life will change. You will love the feeling of accomplishment and the triumph of victory. The journey is on, and I'd love to hear about it! Reach out to me on Facebook—Linda Crawford Books. You cannot change your past, but you can definitely change your future.

Made in the USA
Middletown, DE
13 May 2018